JAZZ & BLUES

Routledge Popular Music

A series of books for schools edited by
Graham Vulliamy and Edward Lee

Jazz & Blues

Graham Vulliamy

Routledge & Kegan Paul
London, Boston and Henley

First published in 1982
by Routledge & Kegan Paul Ltd
39 Store Street, London WC1E 7DD,
9 Park Street, Boston, Mass. 02108, USA and
Broadway House, Newtown Road,
Henley-on-Thames, Oxon RG9 1EN
Set in 11/14pt Helvetica by Input Typesetting Ltd, London
and printed in Great Britain by St Edmundsbury Press,
Bury St Edmunds, Suffolk

ISBN 0–7100–0894–5

For Valerie

Contents

Maxwell Street
Market

1 Introduction

As long ago as 1956, Chuck Berry, one of the
fathers of rock 'n' roll, sang 'Roll over Beethoven, tell
Tchaikovsky the news.' He was pointing to the
enormous difference between 'classical' music and
the kind of pop music that has gripped young people
since the rock 'n' roll explosion of the 1950s.

It's difficult to know what Beethoven, or any of the
other great 'classical' composers, would have made
of it all. Certainly they would have had great difficulty
in understanding today's pop. Think of some of the
differences. Instead of the traditional instruments of
the orchestra, we have electric instruments (guitars,
keyboards and others) capable of playing at limitless
volume. The smooth, controlled voice of the opera
singer gives way to the rough, strained sound of the
rock vocalist or blues singer. And the furious
battering of percussion, highlighted by the wall of
drums and cymbals surrounding the group's
drummer, is a constant reminder of the vital role that
rhythm plays in today's pop. Gone are the sheets of
music from which the classical musician plays. Gone
also is the composer who wrote the music and the
conductor whose job it is to help interpret it. Instead,
the rock musician plays by ear, composing as he is
performing; he plays in a style that he has learned
after listening to endless records and after practising
with fellow musicians.

(top) The Royal Philharmonic Orchestra. (bottom) Howlin' Wolf and his band in a Chicago nightclub. Compare the very different atmospheres at these two musical performances

Our composer would find other differences too, besides the musical ones. Classical music tends to be played in concert halls, opera houses or churches; the audience sit quietly, reserving their applause till the music ends. Pop musicians play in clubs, pubs, the local village hall, but not to a quiet, seated audience. People dance, talk, they often scream and shout; they drink, they may even talk to the musicians. Even when the great rock supergroups give their concerts to audiences of thousands, people are dancing – *moving* to the music.

All of this would show our classical composer that something dramatically new had happened to music. He would want to know how and why there had been this change. He would also no doubt be interested to know why young people today are more interested in music than ever before. For, judging by such things as the large sale of records, instruments, and of pop and rock music magazines, interest in music has grown enormously. All over Europe and the USA people listen to the music of live rock groups. Discos beat out a rhythmic pulse to dance to in the absence of live musicians. And not only the Western world listens to this music. It has become truly international.

Yet the beginnings of all this were most unlikely ones: It all started with a group of black slaves who had been forcibly shipped from their homes in Africa to America, where they were compelled to work. They began a whole musical tradition, without which pop music, as we now know it, would not exist. Put any group of rock musicians together for the first time and what will they be most likely to play? The answer is the blues, a development of the music played by wandering black musicians in the southern

JAZZ JAMBOREE '78

21th INTERNATIONAL
JAZZ FESTIVAL
WARSAW
OCT. 25-29 1978

XXI MIĘDZYNARODOWY FESTIWAL
MUZYKI JAZZOWEJ
WARSZAWA
25-29 X 197

Jazz is very
popular in many
communist
countries,
especially Poland
where these
pictures were
taken

states of America nearly a century ago.

The blues, together with related black music styles like jazz, gospel and rhythm and blues, have helped produce some of the best of today's pop. The origins of rock 'n' roll and much of today's rock music lie in the rhythm and blues of the late 1940s. Soul and Motown music, so popular in the discos, goes back to a mixture of blues and the religious gospel music sung in black churches. Jazz, too, has had a lasting influence on popular music. It has even influenced a number of modern classical composers. Thus this black music tradition has had a greater impact on the Western world during this century than any other musical form.

But the story we shall be telling is not only one of the new music. It is the story of a way of life developed by black people in a white society, and of how the changes in their music are reflections of the changes in their relationships with other people. Finally, it is the story of how young people today, of all colours, have found in this black music tradition the kind of music they want to play and listen to. But first, we must go back to the beginning of the story, in Africa, centuries ago.

2 The roots of black music

What made the black music that developed in the USA so different from both classical music and from the traditional folk songs and ballads, which were popular among the working people in both Britain and the USA? The answer lies in the way in which people in Africa, where the slaves came from, learned, performed and listened to music. In West Africa (the most important source of slaves) the main musical instrument was the drum. Groups of drummers would play music that was highly complicated, particularly in its use of rhythm. Africans would sing and handclap as an accompaniment, but very differently from the way in which Europeans were taught to sing. In some regions of West Africa, the music was also influenced by the music of the Arab countries, which lay to the north. There, in addition to drums, Africans used home-made stringed instruments and rattles. These would accompany the singing of people as they worked, and in the many ceremonies which existed in traditional tribal life.

When the Africans came to America, they created music which mixed both their traditional African music and ideas from the European music of their white masters. This was a new type of music, which was no longer purely African in nature. It therefore

Musicians in
Angola, West
Africa

received a new name, and came to be called Afro-American music. But, before describing this, we need to know something of how the blacks from Africa came to arrive in America.

The slave-trade

The moving of African slaves to other countries had begun as early as the fifteenth century, but the first slaves to land in British America were brought to the state of Virginia by the Dutch in 1619. Over the next 250 years something like 1 million slaves were imported to North America and an even larger number were taken to the West Indies.

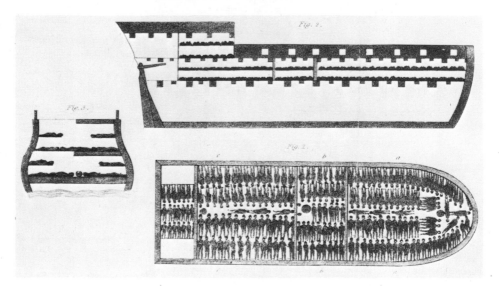

Diagram of slaves packed on board a slave-ship

The slave-trade was one of the most brutal and inhuman aspects of Europe's history. Its only aim was to make money for those ship-owners who, having bought slaves very cheaply in Africa, sold them again in the Americas at a large profit to slave-owners, who would use them to do all the hard labour on farms and cotton plantations. Since making money was the only object, no consideration

SLAVES AT SALE

WITHOUT RESERVE.

BY BEARD, CALHOUN & CO.

J. A. BEARD, Auctioneer.

WILL BE SOLD AT AUCTION ON

TUESDAY, Jan. 16th,

AT 12 O'CLOCK, AT BANKS' ARCADE, THE FOLLOWING DESCRIBED NEGROES :

1. ROSIN, 13 years of age, a griffe, good house boy, fine temper, fully guarantied, and speaks German and English.

2. JORDAN, 23 years of age, a likely negro house servant and trusty waiter, fully guarantied.

3. JANE, aged 24 years, a very superior washer, ironer, good American cook, and House Woman, fully guarantied.

4. MARY, aged 24 years, and child 1 year old, a trusty woman, good washer, ironer and American cook fully guarantied.

5. EDWIN, aged 27 years, a griffe man, an excellent waiter, steward and trusty servant fully guarantied.

6. ESTHER, aged 40 years, a smart intelligent and cleanly cook, washer and ironer, title only guarantied.

7. ANNE, aged 24 years, an excellent house servant, washer, ironer, and good cook, with her three children, one aged 5 another 2 and the last 1 year ; they are fully guarantied but will be sold to go into the country, by her owner's instructions.

8. SAM, aged 28 years, a field hand; title only guarantied.

9. AGNES, aged 24 years, a good cook, washer and ironer, fully guarantied.

10. HENRY, aged about 26 years, a field hand, and a stout man, sold as having run away from the plantation.

11. JOHN, aged 15 years, a smart waiting boy, fully guarantied.

12. JANE, aged 17 years, a fine house girl and field hand fully guarantied.

13. MARY, aged 35 years, superior nurse and house woman, fully guarantied.

ALSO :

14. PATRICK, aged 28 years a likely man good barber, body and house servant. Sold under a good character, and fully guarantied against the vices and maladies prescribed by law.

TERMS CASH. Acts of sale before J. R. BEARD, Notary Public at the expense of the purchasers.

ALSO,

The following described Slaves sold for account of Mr. Henry Deacon, who failed to comply with the terms of sale made for the account of the Succession of C. H. L. ELWYN, deceased, to wit :

The Negress MATHILDA, aged about 29 years and her son PAUL, 7 years-a good washer, Ironer and Cooker.

TERMS CASH. Acts of sale before H. B. CENAS, Notary Public, at the expense of the purchasers.

A poster
advertising slaves
for sale

was given to the Africans as human beings. As a result, the conditions of transportation in the slave-ships crossing the Atlantic were terrible. On many voyages, up to half the total number of slaves died in the ship. They were chained and tightly packed together in spaces of about five feet in length and three feet in height for each person, so they could neither lie down nor sit upright properly. Conditions in the holds were sickening. For weeks on end the slaves lay amid the stench of vomit and excrement, with rats and lice running freely over their chained bodies. While this was considered good enough for the slaves, the slave-masters could not go down into the holds for long without fainting.

Once they were in America they were not treated much better. Many slave-owners treated the slaves just like common animals, often whipping them and even tying them up. In many southern states, laws were introduced to fix clearly what the relationship between slave-owner and slave was. For example,

Slave sale,
Virginia, 1861

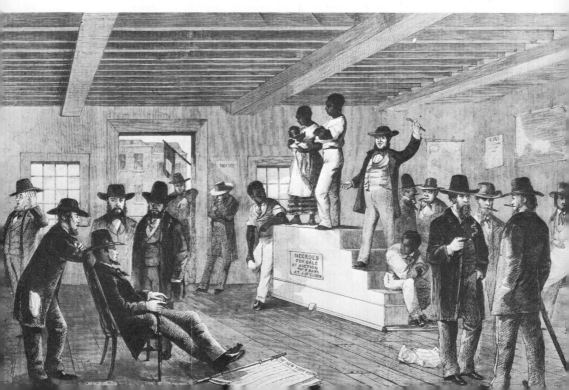

the Civil Code of Louisiana stated that:

> A slave is one who is in the power of a master to whom he belongs. The master may sell him, dispose of his person, his industry, and his labour. He can do nothing, possess nothing, nor acquire anything, but what must belong to his master.

However, it was in these wretched circumstances that we find the origins of the musical heritage that will be the central theme of this book.

Work songs and field hollers

The work song was one of the earliest types of black American music and was strongly influenced by the type of music the blacks had known in Africa. Most of the Africans' traditional leisure pursuits could not take shape in America because the slaves spent most of their time working. Whether on farms or cotton plantations, they were always closely controlled by the slave-owners. Thus drums, which for many Africans were their main musical instrument, were banned in many states for fear that they would be used to start a rebellion and to communicate messages to other slaves at a distance. In Africa there had always been a close relationship between the spoken language and the playing of drums. Drummers could actually copy the rhythm and intonation of speech. In African wrestling, for example, drummers would tap out comments to the fighters – hence the expression 'the talking drum'.

But the traditional African habit of singing to accompany work did not worry the slave-owners because, if anything, it helped the slaves to work harder. The work song usually included a call-and-response pattern of singing. Here one man would sing the verse and the entire group would reply with the chorus. All this would be sung rhythmically in time with whatever work they were doing, easing the boredom. The call-and-response pattern was an important part of the African tradition and later of Afro-American music. It was also important for the development of Afro-American music that the way in which Africans sang was very different from European styles of singing. Africans used varying vocal tones, often involving growls and cries and falsetto, instead of the pure tone favoured by the classically trained singers of Europe.

Work songs were sung extensively on the plantation farms during the days of slavery. Both men and women would be working hard at a variety of jobs, but particularly in helping to pick the cotton crops. They usually sang about their work, but sometimes used the songs purely to express the way they felt about life in general. This included complaining about the way they were overworked, although this could be dangerous if the slave-owners heard them and understood what they were saying:

Well captain, captain, you mus' be blin',
Look at yo' watch! See ain't it quittin' time?
Well captain, captain, how can it be?
Whistles keep a-blowin', you keep a-workin' me.

Later, after the freeing of the slaves, work songs went with the ex-slaves to their new jobs, whether laying rails with a railroad gang or chopping down trees in the lumber camp. Some types of work song have survived even up to the present day. These are mainly in the southern jails, where black convicts sing when doing manual labour in much the same way as they did hundreds of years ago.

Another early black American vocal style which was strongly influenced by African music was the field holler, which was sung by a person working

Cotton picking in Louisiana, 1911

alone, rather than in a group. The holler consisted of a long, wavering one- or two-line call, often in falsetto. It was sometimes used by individuals while working in the cotton fields to communicate with other slaves working in nearby fields. In such cases they would holler in African languages, so that they would be understood by fellow slaves, but not by the white overseers.

Early black religious songs

One of the earliest musical contacts between the black and white people in the south was through religious music. The early nineteenth century was a time of great religious activity in America. Black congregations were particularly attracted to the Baptist and Methodist missionaries, because of their very lively and emotional style of preaching and conducting services. In this, they were closer to African religious practices than any other Christian denominations. However, rather than simply copying the European hymns they heard white people sing, the slaves combined the music and the religious

traditions with those they had known in Africa. Thus
the earliest form of black religious music in America
was probably the ring shout. This was a kind of
religious dance accompanied by singing in a call-
and-response pattern, with the dancers stamping
their feet to beat out a rhythm, as they moved round
in a circle. This illustrates the very different ideas
about religion that exist in Europe and Africa.
European churchgoers sit quietly in their seats, but in
Africa physical action – dance as well as music – is
vital to worship. So also is the call-and-response
technique between preacher and congregation. This
explains the beginning of the song-sermon among
black Americans. Here at religious gatherings, either
in churches or in the widespread camp meetings in
the countryside, the preacher would sing or cry his
line and the congregation would shout or sing the
response.

What are now known as spirituals grew out of the
early ring shouts and song-sermons. To begin with,
blacks and whites worshipped together in churches.
But the whites increasingly disapproved of this, while
blacks were also keen to separate, so that they
could worship in their own ways. Therefore, as early
as 1816 churches were set up for black
congregations only. This meant that, rather than
having to sing traditional hymns in a strictly
European fashion, they could be adapted and sung
with the types of African characteristics we have
discussed. Hymns performed in this way are known
as spirituals. They had a special significance for the
slaves, because they adapted stories from the Bible
to their own situation. One of the most popular was
that of the Israelites in captivity in Egypt, which is the
theme of 'Go Down Moses':

When Israel was in Egypt's Land,
Let my people go!
Oppressed so hard they could not stand,
Let my people go!
Go down, Moses, way down in Egypt's Land,
Tell old Pharaoh, let my people go!

Legend has it that Moses in this spiritual was a
reference to Harriet Tubman, a black anti-slavery
worker who helped slaves escape to the northern
states of America. There blacks were free men,
since most northern states had freed their slaves
early in the nineteenth century or before. Such
double meanings would have been missed by the
whites, who would have interpreted this spiritual as
simply a traditional religious hymn, rather than as a
protest against slavery.

The black religious singing tradition continues to
this day in the form of gospel music, the music of the
black churches. For many of the jazz and blues

Baptist church
congregation,
Atlanta, Georgia

artists we will be meeting later in this book, singing as children in such church choirs and congregations was their first encounter with Afro-American music.

The birth of the blues

No one knows precisely when the blues began. It is almost impossible to tell, because it is difficult to know where the blues begins and other styles of music (like work songs, field hollers and spirituals) end. However, it does seem that some changes in this music were brought about by the freeing of the slaves in 1865. The 'Emancipation of the Slaves', as it was called, came as a result of a civil war between the northern and southern states of America – a war in which the south was finally defeated. The day of freedom, so eagerly awaited by all the black slaves, had arrived at last. But when it came, it did not seem to make much difference. What use was freedom when the ex-slaves had no jobs, nor decent homes and schools? For laws were soon passed to ensure that blacks stayed at the bottom of the economic and social ladder.

Many of the freed slaves moved from the south to other parts of America to build up black communities in the north and west, in cities like Chicago and Kansas. But the vast majority stayed in the south where, thirty years after their emancipation, life was not very different. Most of them were involved in the same kind of agricultural work as they had been as slaves. However, they did have more free time on their hands and were no longer subject to the very strict control of the slave-owner. Perhaps this partly explains why it was during this period, in the second half of the nineteenth century, that we see a rapid development of black music styles. These ranged far beyond the work songs, field hollers and spirituals which had existed in slavery times. And, as in these earlier styles, we find the influence of both African music and the traditional music of white Americans (such as folk songs and hymns) that had been brought over from Europe.

A case in point is the black ballad. The ex-slaves had heard white people sing old European ballads and folk songs and so they adapted these to suit themselves. Some of the most famous black ballads emerged out of the earlier work songs: 'The Ballad of John Henry' was the story of a black steel-driller working on the building of a railway tunnel in 1872. He was supposed to have had a competition with a steam-driven pile driver and beaten it, but, having worked so hard in the attempt, he had a heart attack and died at the moment of victory. This song was originally used as a work song by black workers engaged in railroad-track laying. But it became so famous mainly because it was an example of the black man fighting against almost impossible odds, and it developed into a ballad that was sung by not only black musicians, but white ones too. And each time it was sung, the musician would add to the story, so that John Henry became one of the legends of black history. But the ballads were not always about black heroes like John Henry; they were often about 'bad' men too – songs like the one about Stackerlee, the Memphis City gambler who shot down another black man, called Billy Lyons, after a fight over a Stetson hat.

Ballads weren't the only European musical style to be changed by black people. Traditional dance tunes were played by those slaves who had been allowed to play the fiddle or banjo by their slave-owners. But they were played with the strong rhythmic emphasis that is a basic feature of African music. Hence work songs, field hollers, spirituals, ballads and dance tunes all contained aspects of both African and European music, when they were played or sung by the ex-slaves. These musical forms all affected each other to give a particular black folk-music style. Out of this came the blues.

The blues emerged in order to express the personal feelings of the singer. The ballad told the story of someone else; the work song sang rhythmic phrases designed to coincide with the pace of work; and the spiritual had religious lyrics. But the blues simply expressed the mood of the singer. It gave musicians a chance to talk about themselves: their loves, their hates, their attitudes to work and so on. As the blues singer, Brownie McGhee has put it: 'I don't write anything from imagination. Blues is not a dream. Blues is truth. I can't write about something I haven't seen or experienced.'

One of the musical aspects to influence deeply the development of the blues was the introduction of the guitar, which became more available in the second half of the nineteenth century. Until then the most popular instrument for the slaves and ex-slaves had been the fiddle and the banjo, but the guitar was a much more suitable instrument to accompany the blues singer. This was because the guitar had an almost vocal quality. A player could 'bend' notes in and out of tune by pushing strings sideways out of their normal position, making the guitar sound like a vocal cry. This was a development of a special feature of African music – the 'talking' instrument. In this early music we can observe what is still an important point about black music and much pop music today. Because the music imitates the voice and even sounds from the outside world (such as a train), black musicians seek to get a wide variety of sounds from their instruments. They also like to use instruments whose quality of sound (or timbre) is very different from that which we are used to hearing from orchestral instruments. In fact, the sound of black musicians' instruments is often very harsh to European listeners. This was always true of African music, but was a preference that also came out of necessity in that most of the earliest blues musicians made their own instruments out of everyday materials. For instance, Big Bill Broonzy tells of making a fiddle out of a cigar box and a guitar out of goods boxes when he was only ten years old, while Gus Cannon made his first banjo out of a combination of an old guitar neck and his mother's tin baking pan! Blues singer Robert Pete Williams describes his first instrument in a more detailed way: 'I made my first guitar. I made it out of a cigar box and a good stout long board, and it had five strings of baling wire. Hurt my fingers on it. That was when I was just a farm boy.'

The blues has always been an improvised music – that is, the musician makes up the melodies he plays as he goes along. The earliest blues musicians would also have made up the words as they went along, rather as if they were simply talking to themselves about the way they felt, playing the guitar at the same time. This explains why the structure of blues lyrics often takes the form of one line which is then repeated, followed by a final line – the musician, while repeating the first line, has enough time to think of a final punch line:

Don't leave me baby 'cause I'm so down and blue
No don't leave me baby 'cause I'm so down and
   blue
Deep down in my heart, baby, my love is only for
   you.

Certain features of the blues show the influence of its African origins. After each vocal line will come a short, instrumental guitar break. This highlights the call-and-response pattern so often found in African music, where in this case the vocal acts as the call and the guitar break as the response. The great range of vocal tones used by the singer is similar to African, rather than European, styles of singing. The bending of notes on the guitar is a technique used by stringed-instrument musicians in the Savannah regions of Africa. The way in which the musician sings and plays around the rhythmic beat, rather than on it, is also of African origin; so also is the great stress on repetition, to build up tension and excitement.

But, despite all these African elements blues was still not an African music. In fact, American blues musicians who have visited Africa recently have been amazed at how different African music sounds. For while the slaves might originally have come from Africa, their descendants have been brought up in an entirely different environment – one that has been greatly influenced by American life. Thus, as we have seen, all the black styles of music that developed during and after slavery were *combinations* of African and European musical influences. With the blues the greatest European influence was the harmony, that is the use of chords (such as those strummed by a guitarist) to accompany a melody. The type of harmony, which has dominated classical music for hundreds of years, was unheard of in Africa. This became more apparent when groups of musicians wanted to play the blues together, because, with more than one musician improvising, there had to be some agreed plan or musical structure.

Big Bill Broonzy in a nightclub singing 'the old blues that I learned in Mississippi'

To begin with, three chords were used and arranged in a set order, or sequence. Normally one bar (that is, a count of four beats) would be taken up with one particular chord. The earliest blues probably took the eight- and sixteen-bar forms characteristic of ballads and spirituals, but soon a sequence of twelve bars became the most common. Each of the three lines of the lyric then takes up four bars, although the musician is likely to sing only for the first two of them and then respond with a guitar break for the remaining two. However, as we will be finding out later, the extent to which this twelve-bar blues form is strictly adhered to depends very much on the type of music being played. Whereas jazz musicians playing the blues stick very closely to this structure, using the chords in a definite pattern and for a fixed number of beats, the earliest country blues singers varied it enormously and in many cases were not aware of playing the European-sounding chords at all. As Big Bill Broonzy has said:

> To really sing the old blues that I learned in Mississippi I have to go back to my sound and not the right chords as the musicians have told me to make. They just don't work with the real blues . . . the blues didn't come out of no book and them real chords did.

Ragtime

All the music we have discussed so far has been vocal. However, before we can look at the origins of jazz in the next chapter, we need to look at the first Afro-American instrumental music. Emerging at about the same time as blues, was what came to be called ragtime. Although it was most popular in the first twenty years of the twentieth century, its origins go right back to the 'rags', which were dances developed in black minstrel shows. These had been an important part of the life of the south of America since around 1840. Originally, the minstrel show was a white imitation of black music, dancing and entertainment. Its beginnings are described in more detail in both Edward Lee's *Folk Song and Music Hall* and John Shepherd's *Tin Pan Alley*. White entertainers would black their faces with cork and would make fun of black people. But once the slaves had been freed, they too formed their own minstrel groups, who would try and outdo the white musicians and dancers at their own game – by making fun of the whites making fun of the blacks! They proved a great hit and the minstrel shows became extremely popular during the second half of the nineteenth century.

These black minstrel shows, together with the

travelling carnival shows and circuses, were a
training ground for many great blues and jazz
musicians, who started off in the 'jug' bands
accompanying dancers in the shows. They also did
much to spread black entertainment, and hence
black music, around the south and midwest. And it
was these shows that, in the 1890s, popularised the
new ragtime music to such an extent that it became
a national craze. This was because this new music
was used to accompany a dance called the
'cakewalk', which had become an important part of
any minstrel show. The cakewalk consisted of
couples walking around kicking their legs high in the
air, waving their canes, bowing low and generally
prancing about. It had originally been a dance
developed by the slaves as a take-off of the
exaggerated manners of the high-society white folks.
It came to have such an odd name because, at the
end of a dance session, couples would compete in
front of a panel for the prize of a large plum cake!

But what exactly was ragtime? In its best-known
form it was a style of piano music, which was used
to accompany rag dances or simply played to
entertain in saloon bars, pool halls or restaurants. It
is a piano style, in which the left hand beats out a
steady march-like rhythm and the right plays a faster
and more complicated line of notes, which appears
to 'cut across' the left-hand rhythm. This effect is
called syncopation and gives the music a strongly
rhythmic flavour.

A black musician called Scott Joplin, from St Louis
in the midwest of America (the main centre of
ragtime), helped to make ragtime famous. He had
had a training in classical music and could therefore
read and write down music. He found that ragtime,
unlike the blues, could be written down in musical

form. This enabled his music to become popular with white people, most of whom learned to play by means of written music. Joplin composed many famous rag tunes such as 'Maple Leaf Rag', published in 1899, and 'The Entertainer'. Influenced by his classical training, Joplin tried to relate the two musics. Thus, some ragtime compositions used the forms and harmonies of light classical music. Scott Joplin even went on to compose an opera!

Of the black music styles we have met so far, ragtime is the most European and least African in its origins. But perhaps because of this, it has had a great influence on the white-owned, more commercial side of popular music throughout this century. As it was written down, it could be printed in the form of sheet music, which was the main source of income for popular music publishers. Although ragtime itself faded out after the First World War, its spirit lived on. John Shepherd, in *Tin Pan Alley*, explains more fully how ragtime influenced the popular music industry. 'Tin Pan Alley' was the popular name for the music publishing industry in New York which, until around 1955, was the main provider of the USA's popular music for white people. Song writers in Tin Pan Alley would write music and lyrics so that they could make a lot of money by having them performed by the most famous white singers and bands of the day.

Barrelhouse piano and boogie-woogie styles

However, ragtime was not the only piano style to develop at the end of the last century. At about the same time a style which was much closer to blues music was developing in the lumber camps of Texas and Louisiana, which lay at the heart of the USA's timber industry. Blacks would work sawing down timber in these camps, deep in the forest and miles from anywhere, often connected to other logging camps only by railroads. Life was hard and rough in such places and the only entertainment available was the barrelhouse party on Saturday nights. The barrelhouse would be a beaten-up old shack, which housed plenty of barrels of drink. The place would go mad, so that all the frustrations of the dangerous week's work could be let out – with drinking, gambling, women and dancing. Originally blues guitarists entertained, but soon they found that pianists were better because they could play louder and with a more percussive and rhythmic feel – a sound that was all the more earthy and basic due to the use of old out-of-tune pianos.

So developed the barrelhouse piano style of playing, later to blend into what has been a major influence on later jazz and blues – a style called boogie-woogie. Whereas ragtime was strongly influenced by European classical music, barrelhouse piano was much closer to African music. In fact one famous blues historian has noted the great similarity between barrelhouse piano and West African xylophone techniques, where short rhythmic phrases are set off against each other. By repeating one rhythmic phrase and then another, an excitement is built up in the music. All African instrumental music is percussive, and strongly rhythmic, copying the use of drums. The barrelhouse pianist also played percussively with his interest much more in the rhythm than in the melody – an approach at that time unheard of in classical music.

The logging camps were for many travelling musicians one of the few places they could regularly earn a living. So, many musicians – blues singers, guitarists, pianists – would play the barrelhouse circuit, just as rock bands today talk of playing the college or club circuit. But it was a hard life – as one old musician has put it: 'some of them died real young – and some lived to be thirty-five or forty.' Many, however, learned their trade as blues musicians and then moved off to better things in the cities. Some of the great names of blues and jazz that we will be meeting later in this book (such as Jelly Roll Morton or Blind Lemon Jefferson) had done their turn entertaining in the logging camps.

Conclusion   This has been only a brief survey of some of the major developments in black American music in the nineteenth century. But it has been enough to serve as a backcloth to the growth of the important musical traditions of jazz and blues which have flourished ever since. While we are unsure about exactly how blues began, we can be much more certain about the beginnings of jazz. For this we must look to a bustling port, full not only of whites and blacks but of French, Mexicans, Spanish, Indians and all shades and types in between – the exciting city of New Orleans.

3 The deep south

The birth of jazz New Orleans has often been called the birthplace of jazz. It was an unusual city by American standards. A port, built in a loop of the river Mississippi, it had started as a French city and was then handed over to the Spanish in 1763. Later, it returned to French rule and was finally acquired by America in the Louisiana Purchase of 1803. During the years that followed, New Orleans developed into something of a boom town and the most important port of the southern states of America.

Its European origins explain much of what made the city unusual. For a start, New Orleans had always been much more tolerant towards black people than other parts of the southern states. Also the split between whites and blacks was not as obvious because of the large Creole population. The Creoles formed a bridge between the two communities because they were descended from a mixture of black slaves and French and Spanish people, and thus did not have very dark skins. This group proved very important in the development of jazz. Before the Civil War, they had considerable prestige as a social group; they were well educated and such education often included a training in classical music. The Creoles even had their own opera house in New Orleans, with a conductor who

A New Orleans
street parade

was famous in Europe as well as America. But after
the Civil War, the effect of new laws to segregate –
or forcibly separate – anyone of African ancestry
finally hit the Creoles. They found themselves
pushed out of their good jobs and forced to mix with
the darker-skinned ex-slaves.

The beginnings of jazz were very much a product
of this mixing – a combination of the African musical
traditions of the black ex-slaves, which we traced in
chapter 2, and the European classical musical
interests of the Creoles. Creole musicians had
always played a major part in the New Orleans
tradition of military band music. Brass bands were
used for street parades, picnics, dances, concerts
and even funerals, and the music was a copy of the
white man's march music. However, towards the end
of the nineteenth century, the influence of black
musicians in such bands became greater. They
began to 'jazz' up the marches by playing them in a
more African-inclined style. Thus the emphasis of the
rhythm shifted from the strong to the weak beat and
musicians began to improvise their own melodies,
just as blues musicians had started to improvise.
This produced greater variation in the music and
added colour and excitement.

The process of change from brass band music into
the earliest jazz is best shown by looking at one of
the first New Orleans jazz musicians. Buddy Bolden
was born in 1868 and was brought up in the middle
of the brass band craze, learning to play the cornet
(a small trumpet). But by the end of the nineteenth
century he had taken over many of the other musical
influences around him – ragtime, blues, march music
and even French dance tunes like quadrilles. It was
in the 1890s that he organised his first real jazz
band, although the word 'jazz' itself was not to be

coined till much later. His band consisted of cornet, clarinet, trombone, guitar, bass and drums. It probably developed a jazz style because neither Bolden nor his other musicians could read music. This forced them to improvise and to adapt the techniques of blues guitarists and singers to the brass instruments. This explains the reputation Bolden had for being the harshest and loudest trumpet player in the city – legend had it that he could be heard twelve miles away on a clear night! By the turn of the century he had been nicknamed the trumpet-playing 'King' of New Orleans. But his reign was not to last long. He had always lived an eccentric life with what seemed to be an overdose of both drink and women, and in 1907 he went mad in a somewhat spectacular manner. While playing in a street parade he suddenly started bashing fellow bandsmen and onlookers with his cornet. He was overpowered and carried off to jail, where he was declared insane. He was then sent to the East Louisiana State Hospital at Angola, where he was kept for the remaining twenty-four years of his life.

In Bolden's day playing music was a part-time job. Bolden himself was a barber and other musicians were shopkeepers or craftsmen like carpenters, bricklayers or cigar makers. But there was one district which gave opportunities for the professional employment of musicians. Storyville had been set up in 1897 as a New Orleans 'red-light' district where the sex business – with striptease, prostitutes and brothels – could flourish legally. Jazz bands were employed to work in the dance halls and cabarets, while in the brothels ragtime blues and jazz pianists were particularly popular. One such pianist was Jelly Roll Morton, a Creole musician who was later to lead one of the best New Orleans jazz bands. It was he who was partly responsible for changing the very rigid, and European-influenced, style of piano ragtime we met in chapter 2 into a much more blues-influenced jazz piano style.

Later critics of jazz were to make much of the music's connections with a vice-ridden area like Storyville. But this is not so much a criticism of the music as of the attitude of white society to black people. The earliest jazz was played outdoors at funerals, picnics and parades, but white people would not often have jazz musicians playing at their dances and parties. So the musicians (particularly the pianists) had to go to the only places where they were well paid – and that was the Storyville district.

Just as today in many English and American cities, black people were looked down upon and had to live in the worst areas in appalling conditions. Times were hard and in a situation where most of them had very little money, and often not even a job, there were frequent fights, often with knives or guns. As Jelly Roll Morton said:

Storyville, New Orleans

Anyone could carry a gun that wanted to, almost; the fine was only ten dollars or thirty days in the market, your job being to clean up the market in the morning. Most of the prisoners ran away, so that the thirty days didn't mean anything.

Perhaps it was because life was so rough and difficult that music flourished the way it did. For most blacks it was the only way they could earn good money as well as bring some interest and excitement to their lives. There seems to have been a very large number of black jazz bands in the city. Most musicians either bought their instruments cheaply from pawn shops or made their own. Baby Dodds, the great drummer, made his first set of drums by 'punching holes in a tin can and using chair rounds for sticks'.

The earliest New Orleans jazz was recorded in Chicago in the 1920s and in the next chapter we will see how the musicians moved north to Chicago. But since these musicians first began playing in New Orleans, this city is seen by most historians as the birthplace of jazz. This sounds as though at the turn of the century jazz was only played in New Orleans. However, this is far from being the case. Not only is it likely that other southern cities, particularly in Texas, contained instrumental street bands playing a kind of jazz, but also that many of the earliest New Orleans jazz musicians travelled widely around the USA.

For example, Jelly Roll Morton began travelling as early as 1904, when he was only nineteen. Within a few years he had been all round the USA – to Chicago in the north, California in the west, south to Texas and to St Louis, the home of piano ragtime music, in the midwest. Like blues singers, jazz musicians would travel around as entertainers. By doing so they would not only spread their music to other places, but would also be influenced by the styles of other areas. Thus Jelly Roll Morton would return from his trips not only, as rumour had it, with the experience of a girlfriend from every major city and that much richer from his gambling at the game of pool, but also playing music which was a true mixture of ragtime, blues and jazz. It was this varied musical background, together with Jelly Roll's Creole upbringing that was later to make him an important figure in jazz history. His major achievement was to bring the skill of arrangement and composition to the New Orleans style of jazz (discussed more fully in the next chapter).

Meanwhile – what of the blues?

Jazz historians have sometimes given a false picture by suggesting that the blues was only important in terms of its influence on the development of jazz. Again this is far from the truth. The blues had different beginnings from those of jazz and continued as a separate tradition long after jazz was born. Certainly at different points in their history blues and jazz have both greatly affected each other. We have seen that jazz began partly because the trumpeter Buddy Bolden tried to adapt the blues sound to his brass instrument. In addition, Jelly Roll Morton's meetings with blues musicians in his travels meant that his later jazz recordings would retain a strong blues feeling. In the next chapter we will also see that 'classic' blues singers like Bessie Smith performed with jazz groups.

The Delta blues

But as well as affecting each other, the two musics went their separate ways. While the new sound of jazz was growing in New Orleans, blues musicians of all types continued to travel around the southern states. They produced some of the greatest of what are called the early rural or country blues musicians. Charley Patton, for example, was born in the little town of Edwards in Mississippi around 1887, and was brought up in the heart of the Mississippi Delta. This is an area of D-shaped lowland lying between the Yazzo and the Mississippi Rivers south of Memphis and north of Vicksburg. The area is well known because it has produced many of the greatest country blues singers and has given its name to one of the main styles of blues – the Delta blues.

Charley Patton was the most famous of the early Delta blues singers. Through his skill as a guitarist and singer he managed to escape the back-breaking work in the cotton fields. This was lucky because Charley was not well-suited to such work, as he was slightly built. So he became an entertainer travelling around playing at parties, dances and weekend picnics. Though he died as long ago as 1934, people still remember him for his clowning, his drinking and his womanising, but above all for his music. He sang not only blues, but also ballads that told a story. These were often based on his own experiences, like his 'High Sheriff Blues' which was about how he had been jailed for drunkenness:

> Let me tell you folkses how he treated me
> Let me tell you folkses how he treated me
> And he put me in a cell there it was as dark as it
>   could be
> It takes boozey booze, Lord, to carry me through,
> It takes boozey booze, Lord, to carry me through
> Thirty days seem like years in a jailhouse where
>   there is no booze.

Or sometimes he sang about big events. For instance, his 'High Water Everywhere' told of the disaster and loss of life caused by the Mississippi floods of 1927:

> Ooooh-uh the water is risin', families sinkin' down
> Say now, the water was risin', airplanes all aroun'
> It was fifty men and children come to sink an' drown.

His style was typical of the Delta blues singers and guitarists. Charley had a deep, strong voice and he also used to groan, hum or even yell in his songs. This was a very African style of singing – closer to the field holler than any other country blues style. His guitar style also had strong African influences, being little affected by European melodies and harmonies. This all led to a very intense and emotional kind of music. This is best shown, perhaps, by the 'bottleneck' guitar technique which is associated with the Delta blues. Charley Patton would slide either a knife or the broken-off neck of a bottle along the strings on the guitar neck, which produced a kind of wailing effect in imitation of the human voice. This bottleneck guitar sound, still used by many blues and rock guitarists today, is completely unheard of in the European classical tradition. It probably goes back to the bending of notes practised by the musicians who played stringed instruments in the Savannah regions of West Africa.

The very intense, earthy and African-based sound of the Delta blues is strongly related to that Delta area. Mississippi had the highest proportion of blacks to whites in any part of the USA and, in the Delta region itself, blacks outnumbered whites by two or three to one. Nearly all the blacks worked in the cotton fields and lived in their own communities

A modern blues musician using a bottleneck on the little finger of his left hand

because of the strong feelings of hatred against them by most white people. In such conditions of almost total separation between blacks and whites, the black community's way of life, including its music, was very little influenced by white music or even the black music of other regions. People rarely left the

Delta. Even Charley Patton, the most famous of the early Delta blues singers, only left his home region a few times late in his life. These were when he made brief trips to the north, where he started recording his music in 1929.

Texas blues   Other parts of America, where conditions for blacks were rather different, developed different types of country blues. In Texas, for example, another large source of early country bluesmen, the proportion of blacks to whites was far lower and the whites' hatred of blacks was not so great as in Mississippi. As a result the earliest blues from that region were usually more relaxed, less intense and less African-based. The greater European influence showed both in the shape of the songs, which were closer to a regular twelve-bar type, and in the greater use of harmony.

One of the most famous early Texas blues singers was Blind Lemon Jefferson. Blues history is littered with famous blind musicians – probably because, having no sight, they depended more on a sensitive ear, and anyway they were unable to make a living working normally. Born sometime in the 1890s, near Wortham, Texas, about eighty miles south of Dallas, Blind Lemon started young, singing for coins in the street. After gaining a good reputation, he was soon travelling around as a wandering blues musician. He then became one of the first country blues musicians to win a recording contract, in 1925. He had recorded eighty-one tracks in Chicago in the north when, after a fateful recording session in 1930 in the depth of the Chicago winter, he tried to walk through the snow to a party since a car had failed to collect him. The next day he was found frozen to death on the pavement, having died of a heart attack.

Like all great blues singers, Blind Lemon Jefferson

sang about himself and his own experiences. His most common themes – poverty, liquor, violence, women, even at times dwelling quite openly on aspects of the sexual relationship – reflected the way he lived. When he sang:

> I stood on the corner and almost bust my head.
> I stood on the corner and almost bust my head.
> I couldn't earn enough money to buy me a loaf of bread.

it was the voice of a man who had known poverty most of his life. It was only in his last few years that he made some money through his recordings. Most of this he spent on drink and women, his only other luxury being a car and a chauffeur to drive him around.

Conclusion

At different points in this chapter we have noted how some jazz and blues musicians had moved to the north of the USA, particularly Chicago where most of the earliest recordings were made. The music itself was born in the south, the blues in the heart of the countryside of states like Mississippi and Texas, and jazz in the city, especially New Orleans. But from the 1920s onwards the influence of the music spread all over the USA, particularly to the north. While only the very famous country blues musicians moved north, mainly to record, large numbers of jazz musicians travelled there. And so what was called the Jazz Age of the 1920s is always linked with Chicago, more than a thousand miles from the music's origins. It is to this great move north that we now turn our attention.

4 The big move north

Introduction

The 1920s are often called the Golden Age of Jazz. These were the years when jazz ceased to be music played mainly by black bands in southern American cities. Many white musicians started playing jazz, and popular dance band music became permanently affected by a watered-down kind of jazz style. Even some famous classical composers, like Stravinsky and Milhaud, tried to use certain jazz techniques in their compositions. So within a period of only ten years or so jazz had spread not only all around the USA, but to many other parts of the world (including England) too. 'Jazz' had become a household word and the music was here to stay.

The migration of blacks

How did all this happen? One of the most important reasons for the spread of both jazz and blues around the USA was the movement of the people who played this music – the black people of the south. The early years of this century saw the migration of blacks, not only from the countryside to the city, but also from the south to the north. Migration is the widespread movement of large groups of people within a country. People can move house for many reasons, but when you are very poor, as most of the blacks were, the promise of a job and better living conditions is usually the most important reason. And jobs were available in the factories of the northern cities, like Chicago and Detroit, especially after the beginning of the First World War, in 1914, when war goods were needed. Meanwhile in the south the money to be made by blacks share-cropping in the cotton fields grew less and less. Things were made even worse by certain natural disasters like widespread flooding in 1915 and 1916 and also by plagues of boll-weevils. This was a small cotton-eating insect, about a quarter of an inch long, which first appeared in Texas in the 1890s. In 1921, millions of these insects ate about half of the entire cotton crop of the south.

So the black people moved in search of work and a new life. Most went by train and for many the destination was Chicago, right on the main railroad, the Illinois Central, coming from the south and west. Between 1910 and 1920 the black population of Chicago rose from 40,000 (about 2 per cent of the total) to well over 100,000 (about 4 per cent of the total). But it wasn't only Chicago – other northern cities like Detroit, New York and Philadelphia had similar increases. In one year alone, in the early 1920s, nearly half a million black workers left the south to go elsewhere.

It must have been a strange and exciting experience for them. But, for most, their high hopes of a better life were to be sadly disappointed. Certainly there were jobs and the pay was much better than down south. However, housing conditions in the black areas grew more and more over-crowded, and many northern whites hated the blacks as much as the southern whites had. So, just as in the southern cities, there grew up separate black communities, forced to live in the poorest and most ramshackle parts of the city, like the Southside in

opposite Black communities in northern cities provided a ready-made audience for the blues

Chicago or Harlem in New York. It was these that became the home of the jazz and blues musicians who had moved north, and it was these communities that provided a ready-made audience for the music.

Chicago in the 1920s

Chicago became the home of many of the great jazz musicians, who had started playing in New Orleans; so the style known as 'New Orleans jazz' was that developed and recorded in Chicago in the 1920s. This was an extraordinary time in American history. In 1919 the Prohibition laws had banned the sale of alcoholic drinks throughout the USA. But all big cities had their cafes and bars where illegal 'bootleg' liquor was sold. It was also a time of large-scale organised crime and gang warfare. Big-time criminals like the notorious Al Capone had more power and control in a city like Chicago than the local politicians or mayor! They had enormous amounts of money to spend and were quite happy to pay jazz bands for entertaining them in the night clubs. These were dangerous times though, and many musicians had dramatic stories to tell of how they literally had to dodge flying bottles or even bullets when playing. The trumpeter Jimmy McPartland, for example, remembers a night at the Friar's Sun, a place popular with gangsters:

> So it was late this night, and we were off the bandstand and sitting in the back, when all of a sudden – bang, boom, bang! Somebody was shooting a gun. Mike Fritzl was the boss there, and Mike says, 'Play, play, fellers'. We weren't all that keen, but the shooting had ceased so we got up on the stand to play and there was the bass fiddle all shot to pieces. One of these guys had shot it into splinters just for target practice!

King Oliver and Louis Armstrong

Some of the most famous recordings in jazz's history were made in Chicago in 1923 by King Oliver's Creole Jazz Band. Christened 'King' because of his great trumpet playing in New Orleans, Oliver had moved to Chicago in 1917. He soon proved himself 'King of Chicago' as well and in 1921 formed his own Creole Jazz Band, which opened at the Dreamland Cafe. It was a terrific success and later made a very successful tour of California, showing again the way jazz was spreading all around the USA.

On returning to Chicago King Oliver heard rumours from musicians who had travelled from New Orleans that a trumpeter called Louis Armstrong was the best New Orleans had ever seen. So King Oliver, determined to have the finest band in the land, sent Louis a telegram asking him to come up and play with him in Chicago. Louis was playing for a funeral in New Orleans when he got the message and remembers 'jumping sky-high with joy' at the thought of joining the great King Oliver. He immediately packed his bags, boarded a train arriving in Chicago at eleven o'clock, and took a cab to the Lincoln Gardens, where Oliver's band was already playing. On getting out of the cab and hearing the band from outside the hall, he can remember thinking 'My Gawd, I wonder if I'm good enough to play in that band.' But he needn't have worried, because soon it was going to be Louis Armstrong who was the real star of the band.

In addition to Oliver and Armstrong on cornets, the band contained the famous Johnny Dodds on clarinet. On drums was his brother, Baby Dodds, who had been persuaded to leave a well-paid job playing in a Mississippi riverboat dance band. Like many New Orleans jazz groups they had a female pianist, Lil Hardin, who later became Louis

Armstrong's second wife. She was the only member of the group who hadn't come from New Orleans, having been brought up in Memphis, where she had studied classical music. Lil has said how surprised she was to find that this jazz band not only didn't play from reading sheet music, but also couldn't answer her when she asked what key they were playing in! Here was a typical clash between classical musicians who played from music and jazz musicians who played and improvised by ear. Both King Oliver and Louis Armstrong had a fantastic ability to memorise and play something quickly by ear and Louis has described how they even made up a blending of the two cornet parts in the middle of a number:

> King and I stumbled upon a little something that no other two trumpeters together ever thought of. While the band was just swinging, the King would lean over to me, moving his valves on his trumpet, make notes, the notes that he was going to make when the break in the tune came. I'd listen, and at the same time, I'd be figuring out my second to his lead. When the break would come, I'd have my part to blend right along with his. The crowd would go mad at it!

This band recorded thirty-seven titles in its historic sessions in 1923, and many people see these recordings as the highest peak of the New Orleans jazz style. They are certainly typical of the style in their use of improvisation and the tone they used, which reflected the blues influence that was so important in the creation of jazz.

The New Orleans style features 'collective improvisation', a term which means that *all* the musicians improvised together within a closely fixed framework. By 'improvisation' jazz musicians mean making up the music as they play. This might be a tune, a backing part, a bass line, or many other possibilities. But musicians cannot play just anything, otherwise it would not fit with what the rest of the group are playing. So the notes that are played are taken from the harmony or chord structure of the song. The musical line played by an improvising musician consists of pitches (or notes) and rhythms. The pitches are taken from the chords, as we have just seen. Rhythms are played over a basic beat – the tap your foot makes to a piece of music. But in their improvisations, New Orleans musicians created a type of rhythm which was different from that used by classical composers or, indeed, by ragtime pianists. This is because in New Orleans jazz, as in most later jazz, *all* the musicians improvised using a constant syncopation. This makes the music very catchy and rhythmic – jazz musicians call it 'swing'.

Eventually the King Oliver band split up. Oliver went on tour to Pennsylvania, while Armstrong and his wife, Lil, went later to New York. Oliver's later bands were hit hard by the economic depression of the 1930s and when in 1937 high blood pressure made him quite ill he could not even afford medical treatment. He died in 1938 and his sister was unable to raise enough money for his grave – a sad end to one of the greatest contributors to original New Orleans jazz.

Louis Armstrong was more fortunate, and launched himself on one of the greatest careers jazz has ever seen. He had been born in New Orleans in 1900. The first band he ever played in was that of his reform school where he had been sent at the age of twelve for playfully shooting off a revolver in the streets during the celebrations of New Year's Eve.

He had played in New Orleans groups and in bands on the Mississippi steamers. But it was his co-operation with King Oliver that really made his name. Then, after a short spell in New York, he returned to Chicago to form his famous Hot Five and Hot Seven groups.

These groups changed jazz history. The music moved from the idea of collective improvisation (in which several improvising musicians played an important part in making a total *group* sound) to that of an instrumental solo by one featured musician while the rest of the group acted only as backing. A series of recordings made from 1925 to 1928 shows why Armstrong has been called a jazz genius and the greatest trumpet player ever. He introduced new varieties of tone to the instrument, using techniques that were also apparent in his singing. In fact, the similarity between his trumpet and vocal style shows how jazz musicians use their instruments in imitation of the human voice. They express themselves through their instruments and this is why all jazz musicians have styles and tones of their own, which are immediately recognisable. Armstrong's solos show a marvellous sense of the placing of notes, creating musical tension and release by a combination of subtle rhythmic and melodic changes. His superb solos on 'West End Blues', recorded in 1928, show how jazz had been transformed from an entertainment music in night clubs and dance halls to a musical art capable of comparison with the finest music in other traditions. This record is regarded by many as one of the most outstanding jazz records ever.

One of Armstrong's greatest achievements was to remain at heart an entertainer loved by the public at large, while also creating at the same time brilliantly

Louis Armstrong

artistic music. This explains why later in his career, when he travelled world wide, he put as much emphasis on entertainment and showmanship as on his trumpet playing. Many listeners in England, eager to hear him when he first travelled here in 1932, were disappointed that he spent so much time clowning instead of playing his trumpet. But Armstrong had always been an entertainer, keen to please a wide audience. So it's not surprising that he continued his showman act, which appealed to a wider public than just true jazz fans. In the 1960s he even got records into the hit parade, singing tunes like 'Hello Dolly'. While such records displayed only a small part of his talent, they still brought a peculiarly individualistic style of jazz singing to an otherwise simple song. Although many musicians and jazz fans didn't care much for his recent, more commercial, work, when he eventually died in 1971 he was mourned by everyone. Jazz had lost not only one of its warmest personalities, but one of its most original creators.

Early white jazz

The Jazz Age of the 1920s was the time when jazz ceased to be solely a black man's music and became a music played and loved by white people throughout the USA and in Europe also. It was a white band, the Original Dixieland Jazz Band, that had made the first ever jazz recording, in 1917. They began in New Orleans playing a rather pale imitation of the black jazz at that time, moved to New York and became a huge hit after their recordings. They even visited England as early as 1919. But by the early 1920s they were back in the USA playing dance music (like the new foxtrots) at the height of the ballroom-dancing craze. What came to be known as jazz by the general white public was very different from the real thing. Dance bands, and groups playing Tin Pan Alley popular songs, were called jazz groups just because they used some of the techniques (such as an emphasis upon syncopation and new instrumental tones) that jazz had introduced. But the main features of jazz, like the improvisation of solos and rhythmic swing, were not commercial enough for large, white audiences. Instead, they wanted tunes they could easily sing and remember, together with a strict tempo for dancing.

The huge impact jazz had on American music generally is also shown by Paul Whiteman's attempt to make it more 'respectable'. Whiteman led a large orchestra that played dance music and a kind of 'symphonic jazz', which tried to combine classical music and jazz. In 1924 he put on a concert at the Aeolian Hall, a classical music concert hall in New York. This featured the American composer George Gershwin's composition 'Rhapsody in Blue'. So successful was the concert that Paul Whiteman became crowned 'The King of Jazz'. Although such a title was ridiculous, since Whiteman's music was a long way from real jazz, it nevertheless helped spread jazz's appeal to a wider white audience. No longer could jazz be put down as simply brothel music or the music of gangster-packed Chicago night clubs. Although it was heard in a watered-down commercial form, jazz had begun to become respectable.

At the same time, however, the spread of jazz, in the form of commercial dance music, was also strongly resisted by many white people. Guardians of society's morals, such as clergymen or teachers, often saw it as a threat to 'civilised Christian standards'. Many traditional classical musicians and critics saw it as an attack on their music. Thus a Mr Clark, President of the Christian Endeavour Society, called jazz dancing 'an offence against womanly purity'. The medical director of a girls' high school, a Dr Richards, was even stronger: 'the consensus of opinion of leading medical and other scientific authorities is that its influence is as harmful and degrading to civilised races as it has always been among savages from whom we borrowed it.'

Any distinctive new style attracts not only strong criticism from more conservative people, but also strong support from more rebellious people. In the 1960s it was the hippies and long-haired young people who were seen as rebels. The rock music they listened to was criticised in a similar manner.

The 1920s in the USA also had their rebels among white youth. One such group was centred in Chicago. Young white musicians would venture into the black parts of town, often entering clubs when they were under age, to hear the black jazz musicians play. These musicians were to become the backbone of a new style of real jazz, which came to be called the 'white Chicago Style'. It developed from both the earliest white Dixieland jazz and the black New Orleans styles. But in place of the relaxed rhythm of the New Orleans groups, there was substituted a more aggressive rhythmic swing. As a style it also introduced a new instrument that had not been used in the earliest groups – the saxophone.

The most famous white jazz musician of this period (and, perhaps, ever) was Bix Beiderbecke. Born in 1903 into a well-off, middle-class family, he first learned to play classical piano, but then taught himself to play the cornet. He learned by listening to recordings of the Original Dixieland Jazz Band and by watching idols like King Oliver and Louis Armstrong. But the style he developed was quite different from a black one. His background in classical music gave him both a great harmonic sense and a softer, purer tone to his instrument. He also had a remarkable technical ability and the power to create marvellous melodies in his solos.

After his death he became something of a legend, inspiring both a novel and a film based on his life. Here was the rebellious white, middle-class youth throwing himself into the music of a black man's culture. Torn between the desire to produce really artistic jazz and the more commercial dance band music, he turned to drink and burnt himself out young, dying of pneumonia when only twenty-eight.

But here also was a musical genius – the first white jazz musician to be admired and copied by fellow black musicians. There is even a story of tears of joy running down King Oliver's face when Bix sat in with his band one night at the Plantation Club in Chicago. The great Louis Armstrong was also full of praise for his playing.

Blues in the 1920s

At the time that jazz was spreading all over the USA, the blues was doing the same. The country blues didn't change, because conditions in the countryside remained the same. But more and more southern blacks moved into cities and moved north as we have seen. This created new blues styles. The barrelhouse piano style, originally developed in the lumber camps, was firmly rooted in Chicago by the early 1920s, where it came later to be called boogie-woogie. And in a city where both boogie-woogie and jazz flourished it is not surprising that pianists developed techniques influenced by both types of music. One such pianist was Jimmy Yancey, who was actually born in Chicago in 1896. He started off as a comedian and a tap dancer, before going to work in a baseball park. But, like other Chicago blues pianists, he spent much of his time playing at house-rent parties in the black Southside section of the city. These parties were a means of finding the rent when money was scarce. Spending a few dollars on illegal bootleg liquor and hiring a good pianist, the host would throw a party and charge a small admission fee. If all went well, such parties would make a clear profit which then paid the rent!

Another example of a shift in blues styles on reaching the city is given by the music of a famous duo, consisting of Leroy Carr on piano and vocals and Scrapper Blackwell on guitar. Their music combined the more primitive feel of both barrelhouse piano and country blues guitar and the more regular and tuneful harmonies and melodies which came from the city jazz and blues of the 1920s. They excelled on their slower tunes, which often had a haunting sadness. Their lyrics had a poetic simplicity:

> I had the blues before sunrise, with tears standing in my eyes.
> I had the blues before sunrise, with tears standing in my eyes.
> It's such a miserable feeling, a feeling I do despise.

Above all they were a team, performing much better together than separately. So when Leroy Carr died in 1935 of a liver complaint brought on from drinking too much bad whisky, his friend Scrapper Blackwell was heartbroken. He too turned to alcohol, stopped performing and recording, and was eventually murdered in an Indianapolis side street nearly thirty years later.

Classic blues

The style of blues that became most associated with the 1920s was that of 'classic blues'. This was a style that directly mixed blues with the jazz that had developed in cities like Chicago during this period. Where the country blues musicians and boogie pianists had been men, the classic blues singers were women. In fact it was the women singers who became the first big stars of blues. It was a woman, Mamie Smith, who, in 1920, made the first blues recording – a record called 'Crazy Blues', which sold a staggering 75,000 copies in its first month. All the earliest blues recordings were by women, but their music was very different from that of the country blues musicians. They were professional entertainers who made their names on the stages of the

wandering minstrel and carnival shows. These shows
set up to perform in large tents all over the south and
midwest, rather like travelling circuses today. Most of
these singers sang with jazz music backing them.
Because of this, their songs had to have a more
definite pattern than those of the country blues, and
the vocals were much closer to a standard show-biz,
popular song style. The lyrics were often written by
other writers instead of being improvised in the
country blues tradition. However, they were always
sung in a strong blues style and usually by women
with very powerful voices. Such voices were
necessary so that they could be heard over the loud
sound of a full jazz band.

The most famous classic blues singer was Bessie
Smith, often referred to as the 'Empress of the
Blues'. She was born around 1898 in what she
herself called a 'little ramshackle cabin' in
Chattanooga, Tennessee. Although she was to
become internationally famous for her singing, she
never forgot her poor upbringing, and many consider
her 'Poor Man's Blues', recorded in 1928, to be one
of her finest records:

Mister rich man, rich man, open up your heart and
    mind,
Mister rich man, rich man, open up your heart and
    mind,
Give the poor man a chance, help stop these hard,
    hard times.

While you're living in your mansion, you don't
    know what hard times mean,
While you're living in your mansion, you don't
    know what hard times mean,
Poor working man's wife is starving; your wife is
    living like a queen.

Bessie Smith   She began in the travelling tent shows of the
south, but then moved on to theatres and bars. Once
she had started recording in 1923, she became
immensely popular all over the USA, capable of
drawing huge crowds at theatres in the major cities.
She sang with some of the greatest jazz musicians
of the 1920s and 1930s and, as a supreme recording
artist, she has left behind some of the finest
examples of blues recordings ever made.

Her life, however, like that of so many of the great
black musicians, was a tragic one. She was an
unusual type of person, with a reputation for being
both tough and somewhat crude, but also for being
very generous and kind. She drank too much gin
and had many unhappy love affairs, including a
marriage that ended in separation. She even died
tragically, after a car crash in Mississippi, in 1937.
Perhaps it was the suffering in her life that helped
give her the emotional power of her greatest
performances. Indeed, another musician has said
something very similar of her singing:

> This was no actress; no imitator of a woman's
> woes; there was no pretence. It was the real thing
> – a woman cutting her heart open with a knife
> until it was exposed for us all to see, so that we
> suffered as she suffered, exposed with a rhythmic
> ferocity, indeed, which could hardly be borne.

Conclusion   The 1920s were a golden age for jazz, and also the
time when jazz and blues came closest together, in
the form of the classic blues. Both musics spread all
around the USA. Chicago, in particular, became the
new home for both jazz and blues. This was because
this city was the centre of the new, rapidly
expanding, record industry. It was records, as much

as movement of black people from the south to the north, which helped the spread of this new music. Mamie Smith's first blues record started a multitude of what were called 'Race Recordings'. These were records by black musicians which proved to have an enormous appeal to other black people (and to some whites, too, particularly the records of the black jazzmen). In the cities the records could be bought from shops, but in the country areas both record players and records were taken around by travelling salesmen visiting people's homes.

But the boom in recording didn't last long. In 1929 the USA was plunged into a great economic depression. People could no longer afford to buy records and many of the leading record companies went bankrupt. Most of the small night clubs in cities like Chicago, in which the jazz groups and blues musicians had played, closed down. This caused great changes in the music itself. It was the end of the small New Orleans-style jazz group and the end also of the classic blues singers. The music that replaced them will be the theme of our next chapter.

5 Depression years

The Great Depression The 1930s saw the change of jazz from a small group music to the music of the big bands that came to dominate the 'Swing Era'. Such a change was largely a response to the country's economic fortunes. Following the stock market crash of 1929, the whole economy went downhill. Banks failed, factories closed down, railroad companies went bankrupt and those workers who were lucky enough to keep their jobs had their wages greatly reduced. By the end of 1932, 12 million people were unemployed – a quarter of the country's total labour force.

Naturally this all had a huge effect on the music. The recording industry, which had done so much to spread jazz and blues in the 1920s, collapsed. By 1932 only 6 million records a year were being sold, as against 104 million in 1927. The first performers to be hit were the country blues singers. The field-recording trips, which record producers had made into the heart of the country in the deep south to find new singers, became far too expensive. Only the established stars could continue to record and, again, only those in the cities living close to the recording studios.

The Depression also caused the end of the classic blues singers. The theatres and small clubs where they performed shut down and the travelling carnival and tent shows also packed up. And, anyway, the New Orleans style of jazz, which provided the backing to these singers, was also dying. Even before the Depression many of Chicago's leading jazz musicians had left to go eastwards to New York. Word had it that the bigger dance bands there were employing jazz musicians as their soloists at good rates of pay. It was the beginning of the big band era.

The birth of the big band

Jazz in New York had always been different from that in New Orleans and Chicago. The white Original Dixieland Jazz Band had descended on New York in 1917. This led to a series of ballroom dancing crazes in the 1920s. Ever since then big band dance music with a slight jazz feel had been the rage. New York's Tin Pan Alley was also the centre of the music publishing business, which was more interested in popular songs and dance music than in jazz.

The large, white dance bands played strict-tempo, European-style dance music in the big hotels and ballrooms. But the black bands in Harlem were developing the beginnings of a big band jazz style. We can see this in the career of Fletcher Henderson, together with his talented arranger, Don Redman. In the early 1920s Henderson ran a ten-piece band. This was only two or three more than the standard New Orleans-style jazz group. But the sound was very different because the extra musicians played saxophones. Instead of the collective improvisation of the New Orleans style the band was split into sections: a saxophone section, a brass section consisting of trumpets and trombone and a rhythm section (containing banjo, tuba, piano and drums).

With so many musicians, it was best to have the music arranged and written out for the musicians to follow. But Henderson wanted a combination of the arranged big band sound and the kind of swinging jazz soloing that was featured in New Orleans jazz. So he employed some of the most famous jazz soloists of his day. Louis Armstrong arrived to play with him in 1924. This created a huge stir among the New York musicians because they weren't used to hearing such swinging trumpet playing. Fellow trumpeter, Rex Stewart, talks about the impact Louis made: 'We had never heard anybody improvise that way – the brilliance and boldness of his ideas, the fantastic way he developed them, the deepness of his swing, and that gloriously full, clear sound. It was stunning!'

Don Redman even had to change the style of his arranging as soon as Louis arrived in order to try and get the whole band to swing as well. The general public didn't use the expression 'swing band' until about ten years later – to describe the popular big white bands like Benny Goodman's. But it was here in Harlem in the mid-1920s that it all started.

The swing band sound was achieved by arranging the music so that the different sections and the soloists could be played off against each other in a kind of call-and-response pattern. As we saw with earlier work songs and gospel songs, such a call-and-response technique takes us back again to African music. So also does the use of the riff. This was a musical phrase played by the band sections over and over again to build up musical tension. Such repetition of musical phrases has always been an important feature of West African music.

Fletcher Henderson's band was famous not only for being the first to adapt swinging jazz to a big band sound, but also for producing some great jazz soloists. The famous jazz tenor saxophone player, Coleman Hawkins, first became well known through playing in the Fletcher Henderson band in 1923. He had had a good musical education from childhood. After learning both piano and cello he switched to tenor saxophone when he was only nine years old. He remembers having his classical music lessons, then playing jazz for the rest of the day. As he went to school in Chicago he had plenty of opportunity to see many of the great New Orleans players in action, including Louis Armstrong.

Coleman played in a style with a very full, fat tone and using lots of blues techniques, such as bending and wavering the notes. He also had a great sense of melody and musical shape in his solos, especially when playing the slow ballads at which he excelled. For nearly fifty years he continued to produce beautiful music. Unlike other great musicians of the 1920s, including even Louis Armstrong, he managed to accept the great changes in jazz styles that were to come later in the 1940s and 1950s.

Duke Ellington   But the most famous big band to start in New York in the 1920s was led by someone who was to become one of the greatest jazz musicians ever – Duke Ellington. He was born in 1899 into a fairly well-to-do family in Washington, DC, where his father worked as a butler in the President's White House. Given this background, he also had an early musical education. This explains much of the difference between the big band jazz of New York and the small group jazz of New Orleans and Chicago. Whereas the latter had been played by the poorest blacks, men like Ellington, Fletcher Henderson and Coleman Hawkins were all part of the rising black

Duke Ellington's
Orchestra at the
Cotton Club

middle classes who were both better off and better
educated. Their music came to reflect this better
education, especially their earlier training in classical
music.

When he was eighteen, Ellington (nicknamed
'Duke' by the boy living next door when he was only
eight) turned down the possibility of an art school
scholarship to play music full-time. He began as a
ragtime pianist playing at house-rent parties and
clubs. Then he collected some musicians together
and moved to New York, in 1922. One of these
musicians was the drummer, Sonny Greer, who
incredibly was to remain in the Ellington band for
another thirty years!

The Duke Ellington Orchestra, as it came to be

called, first became really well known after its engagement at the Cotton Club in Harlem, in 1927. Run by gangsters, this was a famous nightspot that put on an extravagant stage show with singers and dancers. Although the club was in the black district of Harlem, it catered only for a white audience. This audience wanted to come from outside Harlem to see 'primitive' music and entertainment. The theme of the shows was the American black man's background in the jungles of Africa. Such a show would now be thought to be in the worst taste (or even against the law because of its racialist undertones). But the club provided the background to Duke Ellington's very individual style of jazz composition. To fit the 'jungle' bill, Ellington would compose pieces that used the abilities of some of his famous trumpeters to 'growl' with their instruments. While at the time this was seen just as a novelty, it was really an application of blues techniques to brass instruments. We saw how blues guitarists could copy the cries and growls of the human voice by 'bending' the notes as they played them. Ellington's trumpeters, like 'Bubber' Miley and 'Tricky' Sam Nanton, could do just the same. They made it even more effective by holding a hat or a 'mute' in front of the end of the trumpet, as they played. This altered the volume and the tone of the sound as it came out. So, while the audience and publicity agents christened the music 'Ellington's Jungle Style', it was merely a form of jazz that fully used traditional black music techniques.

opposite Duke Ellington's Orchestra at the Odeon, Hammersmith, 1971

Duke Ellington led a big band right from these days till his death in 1974. Some of his musicians stayed with him throughout that period. Harry Carney, for example, the orchestra's baritone saxophone player joined Ellington in 1926 and never

left, dying only a few months after Ellington himself.

Ellington is one of the giants of jazz, and for many he will go down as one of the greatest musicians of this century. His major contribution was to show that good jazz could be produced as much by careful composition and arrangements as by the improvising soloist. But this could only be done by writing music in such a way as to allow his musicians to express themselves individually, since this is the key to all jazz. So Ellington composed with his individual musicians in mind. He knew their personalities and styles of playing so well that he could write music that was applicable to them, but to no one else. Such a method of composition is very different from that of the classical composer. He composes a work to be played by many different orchestras so that it sounds similar in each case. Ellington's compositions only had *his* sound with *his* own musicians. That's why it has been said of him 'Ellington plays the piano, but his real instrument is his band.'

During his lifetime he composed literally thousands of works, ranging from unforgettable, short, popular songs like 'Satin Doll' to short concertos for his major soloists (like the famous 'Concerto for Cootie'). He also wrote longer, more ambitious works, like his musical suite, 'Such Sweet Thunder', which was based on Shakespearean characters. His band was his whole life. People were amazed at the way that, even when in his seventies, he continued to tour, doing one-night stands and travelling hundreds of miles each day by coach between performances. But Ellington's reply was that the day he stopped travelling, then he would age overnight. As he put it: 'The road is my home and I'm only comfortable when I'm on the move – New York is only where I keep my mailbox.' So he never stopped. He was still composing songs for his orchestra in hospital, when he died from cancer on 24 May 1974.

The Swing Era

Duke Ellington's was one of the few large bands that managed to keep playing even during the worst part of the economic depression. One way in which the top musicians could survive was to tour Europe when times were difficult in the USA. Louis Armstrong had a very successful tour in 1932; the Duke Ellington Orchestra first came to England in 1933; and Coleman Hawkins spent most of the 1930s in Europe.

Bands like Ellington's and Henderson's never achieved mass popularity. Their appeal was mainly to jazz lovers only. But, just as the white Original Dixieland Jazz Band had popularised New Orleans jazz by watering it down, in the 1930s the white bands did the same thing. By the end of the 1930s big band swing had become a national craze – with a white clarinetist by the name of Benny Goodman crowned 'The King of Swing'.

In the 1930s Benny Goodman led a large dance band. But he always went for a more rhythmic jazz sound, having been born and brought up in Chicago listening to some of the white, Chicago jazz musicians. His big break came in 1934 when he played on a series of radio programmes that were broadcast throughout the USA. This led to a tour of one-night stands right across the country. But this was not very successful (club owners often complained they were too loud), until they played in the huge Palomar Ballroom, Los Angeles, in August 1935. They were a stomping success. The crowd roared their delight and danced all night to the rhythmic music. Within months this music was all the rage and groups of teenagers would even dance up and down the aisles of theatres where the Goodman band was playing.

The new audience was white, high-school and college students. By the mid-1930s the Depression had eased as far as middle-class whites were concerned. These youngsters had money and they wanted to enjoy themselves. Drink was back again too. The Prohibition laws that had banned liquor throughout the USA were dropped in 1933. So, just as English teenagers went wild about the Beatles in the early 1960s, American teenagers danced frenziedly to the sound of the big swing bands. They queued all day to see them; followed them round from concert to concert, and lovingly collected photos of their favourite musicians. Jazz musicians came to be idolised for the first time by a huge, young, white audience.

That big band jazz could become so successful commercially was one of Benny Goodman's greatest achievements. He did it by using the same 'swing' techniques that black bands like Fletcher Henderson's had used ten years earlier. He even employed Fletcher Henderson as his own arranger and has openly credited his success to this source. But Benny Goodman's early, classical music training led him to cut out the more bluesy elements in the black band's approach. Instead, Goodman substituted a more classically based precision. Whereas the black musicians would 'bend' their notes while playing, Goodman would stick to the 'straight' manner of performance used by classical musicians. In effect, he tamed the black big band sound of its more African-based features, but kept the rhythmic swing. This was just the combination that white teenagers wanted. The Goodman band

opposite Jiving in the aisles to Benny Goodman's Orchestra

fitted the bill exactly between the black bands, who were altogether too weird and different, and the normal white dance bands, which were boring because they didn't swing.

Another of Goodman's achievements was to be the first white musician to have black musicians playing in his band. Lionel Hampton, a black musician who had started playing drums and then moved to the vibraphone, was asked to join Benny Goodman and recalls the effect it had. 'Being with Benny,' he said 'we were able to play for the first time in the finest hotels and ballrooms in the country. It served a great purpose. It was wonderful.' But not all black musicians' experiences with white bands were as happy as this. Roy Eldridge, a trumpeter who had played with Duke Ellington, swore he would never play with a white band again after what happened to him. He could not stay in the same hotels as the rest of the band because even in the 1930s there were hotels for whites only or for blacks only. The crunch really came when he was refused admission at a dance, where he was billed as the star attraction! He tells the story:

> I went to a place where we were supposed to play a dance and they wouldn't even let me in the place. 'This is a white dance' they said, and there was my name right outside, Roy 'Little Jazz' Eldridge, and I told them who I was. When I finally did get in, I played that first set, trying to keep from crying. By the time I got through the set, the tears were rolling down my cheeks. I don't know how I made it. I went up to a dressing-room and stood in a corner crying and saying to myself why the hell did I come out here again when I knew what would happen.

Goodman's band contained some great jazz musicians. But, as the Swing Era got under way in the late 1930s, other bands, like those of Glen Miller or Artie Shaw, moved towards a more and more commercial sound. Musical content was sacrificed to glittering uniforms and show appeal. Vocalists who sang slow, romantic ballads or faster, more jazzy, numbers became the new popular idols – singers like Frank Sinatra and Perry Como. Because such vocalists are major figures in the Tin Pan Alley tradition of American popular music, John Shepherd discusses their work more fully in *Tin Pan Alley*. However, as we saw with some white jazz in the 1920s, the more popular and commercial such music becomes for a large, white audience, the more it has precious little to do with real jazz.

Blues in the 1930s

While swing was rapidly becoming the white man's music, black people in the ghettoes of the large cities went on listening to the blues. But styles in this changed too. With competition from all the jazz clubs in Chicago, blues musicians found themselves creating bigger groups, providing music that could also be danced to. A good example is the guitarist Big Bill Broonzy. He started playing duets with a pianist but, early in the 1930s, added a trumpet, clarinet, a second guitar and a bass to make his famous Memphis Five band. He later added a drummer and the guitarists began to experiment with the earliest kinds of electric guitars. These had nothing like the power and volume of today's electric instruments, but they were enough to raise their sound over that of the rest of the band. This created a more powerful music that was ideal for dancing. It was the beginning of what later became called the 'urban blues'.

Johnny Shines

Just as jazz had to become more arranged and structured the bigger the band became, the same was true of the blues. The musicians began to play to a set pattern, with space given for the different instrumentalists to take solos. Inevitably the music became less personal since each musician had also to fit in with the others. Johnny Shines, a blues guitarist who started out playing country blues but developed an urban blues style in Chicago, explains the difference like this:

> You take a man playing the country blues, he plays just what he feels because he's playing all by himself nine times out of ten, and he don't have to cooperate with nobody. But you take Chicago blues style, when you get up there with a band, you have to play together real tight just like it was any other arrangement. It was different, of course, with country blues, because there wasn't any arrangement. If your bluesman felt like holding a note for nine beats, he held it for nine. He didn't know nothin' about any one-two-three-four.

Not everyone, however, turned to urban blues styles. Once the economic depression had eased, record producers continued their trips to the deep south in search of the best country blues musicians to record. More blues legends were created. They included the famous Robert Johnson, who recorded only about thirty tracks in 1936 and 1937, but they are recordings which many consider to be the finest examples of the Delta blues style. They have a powerful emotional intensity, which reflects the anguished life he appears to have led. Always obsessed by women and his sexuality, he never seems to have struck up a happy relationship. He died in 1938 when he was only about twenty-four –

either stabbed or poisoned by a jealous woman, depending on whose story you believe. But when he was killed, Son House, another great blues singer who knew him well, could only say that he was surprised he had lived as long as he did because 'he'd go up to a girl he saw at one of those dances and try to take her off, no matter who was around, her husband or boyfriend or anybody.'

Kansas City styles

While Chicago and New York were the centres of musical activity in the north and east, Kansas City became the centre of the midwest of the USA. Many black people who had migrated from the south turned up there instead of in the northern cities. So by the 1920s it had a large, black working population which enjoyed good jazz and blues music. From early in the century it had attracted a wide variety of musicians. New Orleans jazz musicians had come there by riverboat, first on the Mississippi and then on the Missouri from St Louis. But many boogie-woogie pianists had also made Kansas City their home, together with some of the country blues singers who had travelled around the southwest. So it's not surprising that the style of jazz that developed in this city was one which was based very closely on blues music. Kansas City was one of the few cities where even the Depression had little effect on the music. This was because the city was run by a group of politicians who were in league with the local gangsters. The ban on alcohol during Prohibition didn't mean much to them and all the night clubs sold drink quite openly. As Sammy Price, the pianist, put it: 'There was no depression for the gangsters. The gangsters were doing well and the jazz bands got jobs.'

When big bands started developing in Kansas City

in the 1920s the black audiences in the dance halls wanted them to play blues numbers with a powerful, driving beat. The result was a style of big band jazz that was much closer to the blues than that of the bands of Ellington or Henderson in the east. The most famous band to emerge from this scene was the Count Basie Orchestra. Basie himself had started off playing the piano to accompany blues singers in Harlem in New York. In 1927 he went on a tour round the USA in a travelling show, but this packed up and he was left penniless in Kansas City. However, this didn't particularly worry him: 'I fell in love with Kansas City because that's where I really found the blues.' Soon he had made a big impact on the music scene there, and joined the best musicians in their all-night 'jam' sessions. These were long sessions where the musicians, usually after their regular dance band work, would get together and play for hours on end for the sheer hell of it!

In the early 1930s, Basie played in the famous Benny Moten Orchestra, a swinging blues-based big band. Then, when Moten died in 1935, Basie formed his own group consisting of many of the other musicians from the Moten Orchestra. The new band made its reputation broadcasting over a local Kansas City radio station. It was here, incidentally, that Basie first received his nickname 'Count' from an announcer who thought 'Bill Basie' sounded too ordinary! They then went to New York where they were a huge hit in 1936. Apart from a brief spell in 1950, the band has been playing ever since – they were the other great big band to match Ellington's. But whereas Ellington's Orchestra had used elaborate compositions and arrangements, Basie's was rooted in a more basic simplicity. While they sometimes used arrangements of popular songs,

Count Basie

Little Jimmy
Rushing

they more usually played arrangements of blues
pieces. These were often 'head' arrangements, which
were never written down but simply memorised by
the musicians. They played with a fantastic swing,
created by one of the finest rhythm sections of piano,
bass, rhythm guitar and drums that jazz has ever
seen – real foot-tapping music! The band also
contained some great soloists like the tenor
saxophonist Lester Young, whose marvellously
relaxed, yet swinging, solo style was to influence
many later modern jazzmen. Their close link with the
blues was emphasised by their singer 'Little' Jimmy
Rushing (called 'Little' as a joke, because he was
enormously fat! His other nickname, 'Mr Five by

Five', was a reference to his shape – five feet square!) His powerful blues 'shouting' vocal style was admirably suited to a large band. But the flexibility of the Basie Orchestra was such that it could also back jazz singers as well as blues ones. One of the greatest jazz singers ever, Billie Holliday, made some of her finest recordings with the Basie Orchestra. Her tragic life, scarred by drugs and rejection, was later to become immortalised in the film *Lady Sings the Blues*.

Conclusion The 1930s were eventful years in the USA. First, they saw the Great Depression and then the big band boom of the Swing Era in the late 1930s. Small jazz groups gave way to large, commercial dance bands and jazz orchestras. Jazz, although only in the watered-down form of the large, white bands, became the new national craze – the popular music of the day. At the same time, musicians like Duke Ellington from the new, better-educated, black middle class were creating a more sophisticated big band music. This combined the freedom of jazz soloing with complex written orchestrations. For the poorer blacks in the city, it was the blues that remained their music. In the night spots of cities like Chicago the music was changed into a loud, exciting urban blues style. For musicians in the mid- and southwest, but especially in Kansas City, there was no such split between jazz and blues. With Jimmy Rushing singing, backed by the Count Basie Orchestra, jazz and blues had merged into one. This happened in exactly the same way as it did with the classic blues in the 1920s, as we saw in the last chapter.

6 Disturbance at Minton's

Introduction   The big bands did not last for ever – the boom ended after the finish of the Second World War in 1945. The war itself had harmful effects on swing bands. Many swing musicians were drafted into the army; petrol rationing cut down on band tours and an entertainment tax caused many ballrooms to close. But, most important of all, the popular big bands of the Swing Era were becoming boring. Their commercial box-office appeal made them all sound the same, with the exception of a few of the black ones like Ellington's and Basie's. Keen young jazz musicians became frustrated simply playing the odd solo in a large orchestra. They wanted something new. So, between them, a group of young black jazz musicians, meeting together for jam sessions in a small Harlem club called Minton's Playhouse, created a new style. At the time it was called bebop, but it was the beginnings of modern jazz.

Minton's   Minton's was just the sort of place jazz musicians liked. Small and somewhat seedy, it had a nice informal atmosphere. There was a bar, a bandstand just big enough to take a small grand piano, a drum set and a few standing musicians, and the food was good and quite cheap. In 1941 the club's new musical director decided to hire a resident group or 'house band', but he also encouraged other jazz musicians to join in at jam sessions. Soon the club had acquired an amazing reputation. Some of the most famous jazz musicians, working regularly in the swing bands in other parts of New York, would pack up their instruments and rush up to Harlem as soon as their band dates or 'gigs' were over. Their big band jobs may have paid them well, but Minton's was much more fun, as musicians could solo freely there and not be worried by the strict arrangements of the big bands. And the music was different. The musical director had deliberately experimented by choosing some way-out younger musicians for the 'house band'. Kenny Clarke, the drummer, had earlier been sacked from a big band for not playing in the usual manner – that is, keeping the main beat on the bass drum. Instead he had transferred it to the top cymbal where he could get a much lighter and more flowing rhythm by playing the cymbal continually with his right hand. Then, instead of playing his bass drum regularly, he would use his right foot simply to 'drop bombs', or sudden beats, on the bass drum. This was done to make the music jerky and irregular, in contrast to the monotonous and predictable big band style.

The pianist who was chosen was equally unconventional. Thelonious Monk had started off playing gospel music in churches, but his real love was jazz. He would sit at home practising on a baby grand piano which took up, as his mother put it, 'most of the living room and part of the kitchen'. There he developed a completely original style, using strange chords that were often dissonant (that is, the notes played were chosen especially to clash with each other to give a harsher sound). He experimented with rhythms and, instead of playing continuously, he would leave short rests in his solos for added effect. Even his manner of playing was weird – his fingers very flat on the piano keys and his head held up at an angle, listening intently to the sounds he was creating.

Kenny Clarke and Thelonious Monk fitted together perfectly. Despite their more jagged rhythms, they really swung, but in a manner quite different from previous jazz rhythm sections. Such a combination naturally attracted other younger black jazz musicians who, fed up with the increasing boredom of big band swing music, were also keen to experiment. So Minton's became something of a battleground, with the older, more traditional, musicians being challenged by a younger group, playing in the new modern style. A brilliant young trumpeter called Dizzy Gillespie would get together with Monk and between them they composed tunes with particularly unusual and difficult harmonies to improvise upon. The intention was to frighten off the more traditional musicians or, as Monk himself put it, 'we're going to create something that they can't steal because they can't play it.' But the eventual triumph of modern jazz needed another jazz genius, comparable in importance to a Louis Armstrong or Duke Ellington.

Late in 1941, Monk and Clarke heard a rumour that a great young alto saxophone player, who had just arrived in New York from Kansas City, was playing uptown at Monroe's Club. There they also had jam sessions after the evening's floor show and cabaret was over. So one night they went on up to take a look. 'He was playing stuff we'd never heard before,' remembers Kenny Clarke. 'He was into figures I thought I'd invented for drums. He was twice as fast as Lester Young and into harmony Lester

hadn't touched.' Between them, Monk and Clarke
had stumbled upon the man who was later to
revolutionise jazz – Charlie Parker, nicknamed the
'Yardbird' or, more simply, just 'Bird'.

Charlie 'Bird' Parker

When 'Bird' Parker died on 12 March 1955, the
doctor who examined him thought he was over fifty
years old. The surgeon who carried out the post-
mortem had four possible causes of death suggested
by the doctor. These ranged from stomach ulcers
and pneumonia to a possible heart attack. In fact,
Parker was only thirty-four. But in his short life he
had had enormous appetites: for food, drink, sex
and the hard drugs to which he was addicted for
over fifteen years. He was also diagnosed as
mentally ill, spending parts of his last few years in
hospitals. Such spells in hospital followed either
suicide attempts or bizarre incidents such as setting
fire to his hotel room one night. By the age of sixteen
he was already married with a child (only to be
divorced five years later), a drop-out from school and
spending all his time playing in night club jam
sessions. Here was a man who truly burnt himself
out young and, given the life he led, it's little wonder
that the doctor commented the way he did at his
death. What is remarkable, however, is that from
such a turmoil came what many would consider to be
the greatest genius jazz has ever seen.

Charlie was born in Kansas City in 1920. He was
brought up in the heyday of that city's intense
musical background – the jazz and blues jam
sessions we looked at in the last chapter. He started
playing a baritone horn and clarinet in the school
band when he was thirteen, but soon switched to the
alto saxophone. Even though he was well under age
he would slip out of his home at night and go and

Charlie Parker on saxophone with Thelonious Monk at the piano

visit the night clubs where his jazz idols were playing. He was entirely self-taught, learning from simply watching the way leading sax players fingered their instruments and listening to their improvisations. His favourite was Lester Young, who played tenor sax in the Count Basie Orchestra. Lester's style was very different from that of Coleman Hawkins, the other great saxophonist at that time, but Charlie was attracted by the way Lester would play right across the beat with a great sense of swing. Lester would also use more advanced harmonies and chord changes in his solos than was usual and play with a peculiarly light and airy sound. This was a great model for Parker. Soon Charlie had bought all Lester Young's records and had memorised all his solos.

The other great influence was the blues, which lay at the heart of the Kansas City jazz styles. Charlie practised at home non-stop, learning to play the basic twelve-bar blues in all twelve major keys. Any trained musician would have been able to tell Charlie that this was quite unnecessary, because jazz musicians only played in a very few keys. But it's lucky no one did tell him and that Charlie had the patience to press on. By doing so, he acquired, quite naturally rather than being taught by theory, the very advanced harmonic understanding that was to help bring about the modern jazz developments.

After touring with a big band, Parker ended up in New York at the age of twenty-one. Soon musicians from all around had heard the story of this fantastic new saxophone soloist, who was playing in a way no one had heard before. This was what had brought Monk and Clarke over from Minton's and it didn't take much persuasion for Parker to move to a club where he could play with other musicians, such as Dizzy Gillespie, who were working along similar lines to him. They laid the foundations of the new style in jazz that came to be called bebop or simply bop.

Dizzy, like Charlie, had both a dazzling technique and a great harmonic understanding. The group would usually consist of sax, trumpet, piano, bass and drums. A number of things made the music quite different from previous jazz. Earlier jazz had used popular songs of the day as a starting-point for improvisations. First, the band played the tune and its backing harmonies. Next, the rhythm section kept playing these harmonies (known as the chord sequence), while a soloist invented new ideas over the top of them.

Bop musicians followed the same basic pattern but made various changes. They used the backing harmonies, but did not play the original tune (this had the advantage of avoiding copyright fees, which are payable on tunes but not on harmonies). Often they would invent a new, more complex and rhythmic tune; this created a better jazz mood than the old, sentimental Tin Pan Alley themes. The rhythm section players would also alter the original chords according to the rules of advanced harmony, so as to bring out unusual and dissonant notes. Soloists would then often pick up these notes and use them in their improvisations. Finally, and most important, all the band was concerned to exploit the new rhythmic feel discovered by Kenny Clarke and Thelonious Monk. They would play faster and more jagged-sounding rhythms.

Such playing required a superb technique, or the ability to handle the instrument, aided, in Parker's case anyway, by an amazing musical memory. The great jazz pianist Earl Hines could hardly believe Charlie's playing when he first joined his orchestra: 'When we would rehearse a new arrangement, he would run his part down once, and when we were ready to play it the second time, he knew the whole thing from memory.'

Parker made numerous recordings – many with Gillespie and many with a young trumpeter called Miles Davis, who later became another leading jazz figure. His finest work was often recorded live, as at a Carnegie Hall concert in New York in 1947, and a concert at Massey Hall, Toronto, in 1953. At both of these he was teamed with Dizzy Gillespie, who, as something of a clown and a showman, was always very popular with audiences. Bird's influence was so great that for years after his death it was difficult to find another alto sax player who didn't sound like just a poor copy of him. But, more than this, he

Dizzy Gillespie   affected all jazz musicians. Perhaps Cootie Williams, a trumpeter in Duke Ellington's band, sums this up best: 'Louis Armstrong changed all the brass players around, but after Bird *all* of the instruments had to change – drums, piano, bass and trombones, trumpets, saxophones, everything.'

Bop and the public

Bop was more than just a musical revolution in jazz, it was also a political and social one. Young black musicians were fed up with the way previous jazz developments had been commercialised by white musicians. They were tired of playing the same old stuff in big swing bands. They were also disillusioned, having wrongly thought that problems of racial prejudice would be solved after travelling north from the south. No longer did they want to entertain large audiences with a kind of watered-down jazz music they did not enjoy playing. Instead, they wanted to create their own music and make it so difficult that the whites couldn't steal it. This was, for the first time in jazz's history, a revolt by the musicians against the public. Thelonious Monk expressed the new attitude like this: 'I say play your own way. Don't play what the public wants – you play what you want and let the public pick up what *you* are doing, even if it *does* take them fifteen, twenty years.'

Musicians were often quite hostile to their audiences. They would turn their back on them while playing and develop a 'hip' style of speech which outsiders couldn't understand. Thus the musicians and a keen group of followers formed a close 'in-group' centred on the new music. Drugs, which must have been partly responsible for Charlie Parker's early death, became an increasing part of the scene. Soft drugs such as marijuana had been widely used by jazz musicians, and black people in general, for some time. But the early 1940s saw an alarming increase in the use among musicians of hard drugs like heroin. These were used both as an act of defiance against conventional society and as a release from the incredible pressures under which the musicians had to work. Such pressures, like playing till the early hours of the morning, were made worse by the jazzmen's new attitudes. They saw themselves as artists, creating a great new music after intensive practice, but having still to play in dingy night clubs with a chattering audience who failed to recognise the jazzmen's art.

Critics' reactions didn't help either: many called the new music non-jazz or anti-jazz. Even some of the greatest established musicians reacted with hostility. Louis Armstrong's verdict was:

> So you get all them weird chords which don't mean nothing, and first people get curious about it just because it's new, but soon they get tired of it because it's really no good and you get no melody to remember and no beat to dance to.

But Louis, although a great musician, was wrong. Within ten years the new sounds that the bop musicians had made had not only become part of the new language of jazz, but had also been accepted in popular songs as well. What had seemed like a complete break with jazz's past in the 1940s could later be seen as a quite logical development. While the new music had flowered at Minton's, the seeds had been sown far earlier, in for example the solos of men like Lester Young.

Modern jazz   Modern jazz has seen a number of different developments since the birth of bop. One of the earliest was inspired by Miles Davis, a trumpeter who had often played with Parker. In 1949 he led a nine-piece group in some recordings that were called the 'Birth of the Cool'. The group contained a tuba and French horn as well as normal jazz instruments; all these instruments were blended together with skilful and unusual musical arrangements. Bop had had a driving intensity, with the instruments often using expressive blues techniques like harsh tones and 'bending' notes. But the cool approach was very different – here the instruments were used in a manner closer to that found in a classical orchestra. Unlike bop, many of the musicians involved in this new cool school of jazz were white and in many cases they brought a thorough training in classical music and orchestration to the music. This led to a whole school of mainly white jazz, centred on the west coast of America, which came to dominate the jazz scene in the early 1950s. Groups like those of baritone sax player Gerry Mulligan and pianist Dave Brubeck became immensely popular, particularly with white school and college students. Brubeck even got a record into the British Top Twenty in 1961.

Cool jazz was also a major influence on the development of Third Stream Music. This was a style that tried to mix jazz and classical music directly, to give a kind of highly educated, composed, type of jazz. A group like the famous Modern Jazz Quartet, led by pianist John Lewis, would not only play numbers based on classical music forms, such as the fugues of Bach, but would also perform together with a classical string quartet playing compositions by John Lewis himself. The results, though interesting, finally failed because they lacked both the quality which had been achieved in the best classical music and the rhythmic drive of the best jazz. For the qualities of composed classical music are very different from those in Afro-American music. Classical music is widely valued because of its expression through often lengthy pieces of music, in which a lot of attention is given by composers and listeners to the way in which music is put together (its form). Because the composer can think very carefully about what he writes, and can reflect upon it before writing a final version, classical music can develop themes and ideas right through a long piece of music.

It was only a matter of time before a reaction set in against this more formal, European-influenced style of jazz. Black musicians wanted to return to the more intense drive of bop together with more basic black influences like the blues and gospel music. This they did in a new style labelled at the time 'hard bop'. Musicians on the east coast (saxophonists Sonny Rollins and Cannonball Adderley, for instance) revitalised jazz in the direction of its black music roots. Pianist Thelonious Monk also came to the fore again, having almost faded out altogether during the years of cool jazz because he had refused to alter his style of playing.

At the same time, the black trumpeter Miles Davis came to show himself in his true light. Although mainly responsible for the onset of cool jazz, he was never happy with the way white musicians were taking jazz along a more and more intellectual path, removing it further and further from its origins in the blues. He retained his somewhat cool trumpet sound, but returned to playing a more blues-based style of music, surrounding himself with some of the best of the hard-bop soloists.

Miles Davis has since become one of the most

important figures in jazz since Parker. His style of trumpet playing has always been very different from that of other great jazz trumpet soloists like Armstrong and Gillespie. Compared with them, he lacked technique and he never played in the spectacular, fiery manner they did. But he had a marvellous sense of structure in his solos, together with a very sensitive, almost poetic, manner of playing. More than any other jazz musician he has been responsible for introducing a number of new styles. In the late 1950s his group was experimenting by improvising on modes, which are different kinds of scales from those previously used in jazz. This gave the music a very different feel and sound. Miles himself described this new approach as 'a challenge to see how melodically inventive you are. When you go this way, you can go on forever. You don't have to worry about changes [chord progressions].' He also teamed up with the Canadian arranger Gil Evans to produce a few classic recordings (particularly 'Miles Ahead' and 'Porgy and Bess') featuring a large jazz orchestra. The music sounded like a cross between the original 'Birth of the Cool' orchestra and that of Duke Ellington. Finally, in the late 1960s, Miles showed his remarkable individuality yet again by being the first jazz musician to use an electric bass and electric piano in his group. By doing so, he started a new trend of jazz-rock groups, which we shall be meeting again in chapter 8.

Free-form jazz Miles Davis picked brilliant soloists to play in his groups; one such musician was the tenor saxophone player John Coltrane who joined Miles's group in 1955. He was later to clear the pathway towards another revolution in jazz, as significant as the bop revolution of the 1940s. Born in 1926, Coltrane was reputed to be an extremely shy and gentle man, with an intensely spiritual view of life, combining aspects of Christianity and those of Eastern religions. He died from cancer in 1967, while he was still young.

Coltrane's musical innovations were many. He fully developed a style of improvising based on modes, which had been started earlier in Miles Davis's group. He used the tenor saxophone to create sounds unheard of before, like screams and growls. He learned to play different notes at the same time on the saxophone (using special fingering techniques) to produce what his fellow musicians called 'sheets of sound', instead of the more usual single-note melodies of a saxophone solo. Finally, he showed the possibility of extended jazz solos – on 'Chasin' the Trane', recorded live at a New York jazz club, he took a short section, or riff, from a blues melody and soloed for sixteen minutes on it, backed only by bass and drums. And yet in no way was the solo repetitive. It continued to build in a totally original and imaginative way to produce a passionate musical climax.

Other musicians were working in similar directions. An alto sax player called Ornette Coleman had started off playing tenor sax in local rhythm and blues bands in Texas, where he was born in 1930. By the age of nineteen he had also played in many local bebop bands. But he found aspects of both rhythm and blues and bebop musically frustrating. In 1949 Coleman moved to Los Angeles, where he spent the next few years developing his new experimental approach to jazz playing. Then, in 1959 when he brought his group to play at the Five Spot Club in New York, the jazz community knew that here was a man who would change the course of jazz yet again. Even the instruments were unusual: Coleman himself played a white, plastic saxophone instead of the usual metal one, because he preferred its tone; his trumpeter, Don Cherry, played a tiny pocket trumpet, supposedly because he could then hear what he played more easily; and there was no piano, only bass and drums.

The most noticeable and immediate difference in the sound of the music was its rhythm. Previous jazz usually consisted of a soloist playing to a rhythmic swinging background provided by the rhythm section of piano, bass and drums. But Coleman felt that these rhythm instruments should also act like front-line solo ones because, now that jazz was no longer used as a basis for dancing, there was no need to have such a constant beat. The music is therefore much freer with all the instruments playing together, often to no set rhythmic structure. Coleman also broke away from both the chord structures and modes that had guided previous jazz. Instead, he would take a theme or melody and change and develop it in different ways with no reference to any harmonic or modal basis. The sounds he produced from his instrument were even weirder than those of Coltrane; he would often play deliberately out of tune to give the music more feel.

This new style, which attracted more and more younger musicians, came to be called 'free form'. This label indicated that the set form or structure on which the jazzmen played had been abandoned. Coleman's famous 'Free Jazz' recording of 1960 is a continuous thirty-eight minute improvisation by eight musicians. It was based on no set theme or structure and was totally unrehearsed. One might think this would lead to musical chaos, but the musicians somehow managed to blend together perfectly, giving an intensely emotional musical performance.

Since then, many other younger jazz musicians have sought to break down previous jazz barriers, and, in addition to free form, this area of music is often called the 'new' jazz or the jazz avant-garde. One aspect that most of these experiments have in common is a turning away from more traditional European musical values (such as the use of harmony), which had become increasingly important in jazz. Instead, the new free jazz was going back for some of its inspiration to the earliest black music, such as country blues and street brass bands. The raw, speech-like cries that Ornette Coleman produced on his saxophone seemed like instrumental versions of the very earliest black vocal field hollers from the deep south.

Reactions to free form

Earlier in this chapter we saw how the bop revolution was a reaction by young black musicians against the over-commercialised and stereotyped nature of swing. The situation of free form was very similar, but in this case the reaction was against the stereotyped nature of modern jazz in the 1950s. Perhaps even more than bop, free jazz was a music of protest and, like bop, its major figures were young black musicians. It was no accident that free form happened at a time when blacks in the USA were getting more and more aggressive in their demands for equality with whites. The Civil Rights Movement of the 1950s had failed to give blacks true equality and consequently many younger black people turned to the Black Power Movement. If musicians like the saxophonist Archie Shepp sound fierce, it is because he is expressing his very strong feelings about the way some of his fellow blacks are treated:

Living conditions for blacks are still very poor in many parts of America. This picture was taken in Alabama in 1979

This is a nation which is at war. A nation which is fighting an unjust and dirty war, and it's all reflected in its art, that's all. You can't blow up three children and a church without it somehow reflecting itself in some aspects of your cultural experience. That's what the Avant-garde is about, I think. We're not simply angry young men – we are enraged. And I think it's damn well time. There has been too much death among us.

At the same time, black people in the USA began to express a deeper pride in their own African backgrounds. It is therefore hardly surprising that the music turned away from its European harmonic influences and returned to its African origins. The earliest jazz and blues musicians had used their instruments to copy the human voice because they had never had any formal training in music. However, for the jazz avant-garde it was a conscious decision to play their instruments in that way. Most of them are highly trained musicians, many having been to classical music academies, as well as having jazz backgrounds. Pianist Cecil Taylor, for example, has had a wide musical training in both jazz and classical music, but, instead of playing the piano in the way trained classical musicians do, he has developed his own highly complex style. His bass player has described it like this: 'Cecil is trying to get the vocal sound out of the piano, and I think he's achieved it on many occasions. You can almost hear the piano scream or cry.'

Reactions to free jazz have been similar in many ways to the earlier reactions to bop. Because the music is often difficult to understand, critics have dismissed it as anti-jazz, even anti-music. When Ornette Coleman first burst on the scene, he was dismissed by many famous bop musicians as a faker, a man who couldn't even play his instrument properly. But, like Louis Armstrong's earlier comments on bop, such views were soon shown to be misguided. Again, one of the most famous 'new' jazz saxophonists, Alber Ayler, described his own music like this:

> It seemed to me that on the tenor [saxophone] you could get out all the feelings of the ghetto. On that horn you can shout and really tell the truth. After all, this music comes from the heart of America, the soul of the ghetto.

But when Ayler brought his group over to England a well-known critic could only say that 'at times the quintet resembled an underrehearsed bugle band.'

Conclusion   The period since the Second World War has seen remarkable developments in jazz, first with the bop revolution and later with free jazz. Jazz ceased to be just 'entertainment' music, music to dance to. The new musicians saw themselves as artists, deliberately extending the musical frontiers of jazz regardless of whether this had popular appeal or not. Some of the best of today's younger black musicians, like Anthony Braxton, have not only had a broad musical training which covers both jazz and modern forms of classical music, but are also highly educated as well. Braxton, who plays a number of instruments, studied philosophy at university and is currently writing two symphonies (one of which is intended to be played by six orchestras!), in addition to all his jazz activities.

However, in the USA the musical achievements of modern jazzmen were rarely recognised. White society was not prepared to admit that black musicians had created a music that could rival European classical music, and that could be considered as a serious art form. Jazz musicians visiting Europe found they were better known and more respected over there than they were at home. This was mainly because European countries do not have the race problem that the USA has. Charlie Parker visited both France and Sweden and was amazed at the reception he received. A number of free-jazz musicians have come to live in Europe since they find that over there, not only are they respected more as individuals, but also their music is better understood.

Sadly, another consequence of jazz in the USA becoming a serious art form is that it lost its previous mass support from the black population. Jazz had become a minority music. But black music remained as important to the mass of blacks as it had always been. What they were listening to were the raw

sounds of urban blues music and rhythm and blues –
after the Second World War these became
increasingly popular in the black areas of large
cities. This continuation of the popular brand of black
music will be the theme of our next chapter.

7 The blues roll on

Introduction
The new developments in bebop jazz of the early 1940s appealed to only a small, black audience. The blues remained the music of the large number of poor blacks, especially those packed into the ghetto areas of the northern cities. This was the music most of them had brought from down south, particularly when they had come from the Delta area. During the Great Depression of the 1930s fewer blacks had moved north as there were no jobs to go to. But this all changed again when the United States entered the Second World War in 1941. Northern wartime industries needed unskilled workers. At the same time, farming down south was becoming mechanised, so that many black workers were losing their jobs to machines. So between 1940 and 1950 over 1.5 million blacks left the south – the largest number in any ten-year period. Mississippi alone lost one quarter of its total black population. It was this enormous movement of black workers that helps to explain the beginnings of the new blues styles that emerged after the Second World War.

Chicago
As before, large numbers went to Chicago. Most of them had been farm workers from the Delta. They travelled up on the Illinois Central Railroad which ran direct from New Orleans through the Mississippi

A black district in Chicago

Delta to Chicago. The music they brought was that of the country blues. Not only did they bring musicians, but also a readymade audience. Soon the blues clubs were full of new sounds – traditional country blues, though played much louder with electric guitars. This was very different from the blues which had dominated the Chicago recording industry in the late 1930s. The biggest record company was Bluebird – run by a white businessman, Lester Melrose. The 'Bluebird Beat' as it was called featured groups of musicians who had either been born in Chicago or who had moved north in the great migration following the First World War. Their music was far removed from the old country blues. They had increased the size of the groups with saxophones and harmonicas, and even trumpets and clarinets. The sound was smoother and lacked the harshness of the old country blues. The blacks who had lived a long time in Chicago preferred it; they did not want to be reminded of the bad old days working in the fields in Mississippi. But the new migrants knew no music other than the Delta country blues and so the scene was set for a clash of styles. The established 'Bluebird Beat' would probably have won had it not been for a dramatic change in the recording industry. In August 1942 there began a two-year ban on the making of records. This was mainly caused by the trade union which represented the musicians. These musicians argued that jukeboxes were taking away their possibilities of work. Too many people were dancing to records, they said, instead of to groups.

When the ban was finally lifted, and the Second World War over, there was a huge demand for new blues records. Companies like Bluebird continued to record their old blues stars. But new record companies wanted to cash in on the boom, too. They needed new blues artists to record. Who better than the flood of new Delta country blues singers who had only recently arrived in Chicago and were playing a style of blues much closer to that of the traditional Delta one? The new independent record companies were owned and controlled by blacks. Many of them began in basements or garages. Soon such companies had attracted the blues market of the established giants like Bluebird and Columbia. The new post-war sound was that of Chicago 'downhome' blues – a reference to the singers' recent homes down south. The most famous of the new companies was Chess Records and its big new star was Muddy Waters.

Muddy Waters   Born and brought up in Mississippi, Muddy Waters started playing harmonica, but when he was seventeen switched to guitar. He played in a bottleneck style, learning from the famous Delta blues musicians like Charley Patton and Robert Johnson. Times were bad in Mississippi in the 1930s and, having married at only eighteen, Muddy was having to work hard in the cotton fields to keep his wife and himself. Knowing he could make it as a blues musician in the right environment he finally decided, at the age of twenty-eight, to pack up his bags and go with his wife to Chicago. This was in the middle of 1943 and since it was wartime he found little difficulty in getting a job.

In a short time he had built up quite a reputation playing at house-rent parties, but once he started performing in the small clubs he had a problem – 'You can't hear an acoustic in a liquor club. There's just too much noise,' he said. This was solved when, in 1945, his uncle gave him his first electric guitar. Soon he was being recommended to the talent scouts of Chess Records and in 1946 he went into the studios to record his first tracks for them.

He was an instant success. His records sold well enough for him to be able to give up his daytime factory job. To begin with he was recorded singing and playing a wailing bottleneck guitar, accompanied only by a string bass. Then, in 1950, the brilliant young harmonica player, Little Walter, joined him on records. The blues harmonica, or harp (short for mouth-harp) as it was often called, had been developed by the great John Lee 'Sonny Boy' Williamson. Working with bands like Big Bill Broonzy's in the late 1930s and early 1940s, Sonny Boy would interchange vocals and harmonica breaks to build up a continuous melodic line (singing first, then carrying on the tune with his harmonica). He was destined to become one of the all-time blues greats, but, in 1948, when only thirty-four, he was

Musicians playing in Maxwell Street Market

brutally murdered while walking home in the middle of the night. The murderer made off with his wallet, wrist-watch and three harps.

Little Walter carried on Sonny Boy's tradition of blues harp playing and made this instrument one of the central ones in the Chicago blues band sound of the early 1950s. But Little Walter was yet another example of a musical genius who burnt himself out young. When only eight years old, he had helped earn a living from his harmonica playing by begging on the streets. When at seventeen he came to Chicago, he was discovered by the blues singer Big Bill Broonzy playing in the famous Maxwell Street Market. This was an area of the Southside black district of Chicago, where musicians would get together and play to impress the crowds wandering around the street-market. In the old days the musicians would just use acoustic instruments which presented no problem. However, with the increase in electric instruments, the musicians had to rent a power line from the nearby houses so they could play! Broonzy introduced Little Walter to Muddy Waters and soon they were both recording together, making Little Walter a recording star at the ripe old age of seventeen. His career, however, was short-lived. He died in 1968 at the age of thirty-seven, having spent the last half of his life drinking heavily, so losing his reputation as the greatest harp player in Chicago blues.

All his fellow musicians agreed on Little Walter's talent. Bluesman Howlin' Wolf has said:

> He could have been the biggest. I don't like to say nothin' about nobody, but that boy could have been tops in the blues field. . . . Too much of that liquor and too much of that other stuff, that pot and stuff, brought him down.

Little Walter introduced a whole new way of playing the harmonica, using sudden swooping moans and a big full sound that, although he was amplified with a microphone, seemed impossible coming from such a small instrument. But, above all, he had a marvellous musical sense, always knowing when to blow hard in an attacking way and when to play softly as a subtle background to another musician's solo. Muddy recognised Little Walter's talent immediately he met him and has always been saddened by the way he went downhill:

> When I met him he wasn't drinking nothin' but Pepsi Cola. Just a kid. And I'll tell you, I had the best harmonica player in the business, man. He put a lot of trick things in there, getting all different sounds, man he was the greatest. He always had ideas.

Muddy Waters
and his Band

Muddy himself went on to become *the* great Chicago blues musician. The mid-1950s were the boom time for Chicago City blues, when the top bands could play regularly seven nights a week in the clubs. A typical line-up would be two guitars, harmonica, piano, bass guitar and drums, and the emphasis was very much on volume. Apart from his deep voice and slide-guitar work, Muddy's continual success could be put down to his knack of getting some of the best musicians to play in his band. Many, like Little Walter, soon left to lead their own groups, but others, like Muddy's half-brother, pianist Otis Spann, stayed with him for a long time.

Muddy's best year was 1954. By then his music had changed, moving away from just a straight electric amplification of traditional Delta blues towards a louder, more regularly rhythmic sound. His vocals needed to be stronger, even shouted, to rise over the rest of the band, while the drummer provided a strong backbeat. A good example is the record 'Hoochie Coochie Man', which sold 4,000 records in its first week of release and later became Muddy's biggest ever hit. It was written by Willie Dixon, who often played bass in Muddy's band and who went on to become one of the most important composers and record producers on the Chicago post-war blues scene. The song's theme was a rather weird mixture of magic and superstition on the one hand, and sex on the other. Muddy's approach to sex, a common theme in his lyrics, was an aggressive, male-dominated one, which seemed to reflect the aggressive nature of the music he played. He would often disguise his sexual references in other terms, but to his audience the meaning would be quite apparent:

I can raise your hood
I can clean your coils
Check the transmissions
And, give you the oils
I don't care what the people think
I want to put a tiger, you know, in your tank.

Other blues centres

Chicago was not the only city to update the country blues to give a tougher, electrically amplified sound. The northern city of Detroit became the home of another famous post-war blues singer to work in a similar style. John Lee Hooker was born in Clarksdale, Mississippi, where Muddy Waters was brought up. He learned the guitar from his stepfather who was a friend of both Charley Patton and Blind Lemon Jefferson. After moving north to Detroit, Hooker played the clubs in a similar way to Muddy, although using a smaller group of only four musicians.

But in other areas of the USA, completely different blues styles were developing. The difference in styles can best be explained by looking at the different paths taken by the black migrants. We have seen how most of the rural Mississippi workers who moved went to Chicago. Consequently the Chicago post-war blues style was the old Delta one, amplified by the use both of electric instruments and of larger groups, to suit the new city audiences. We saw, however, in chapter 3, how a different rural blues style emerged in Texas. Musicians like Blind Lemon Jefferson played in a more relaxed and less African-based style. Now, when the black workers migrated from states like Texas, they usually went to the west coast of the USA rather than to the north. Unlike the moves north, the large moves to the west didn't occur until the 1940s. In this decade the black population of California increased by nearly one-third of a million to 462,000. Los Angeles, with plenty of work for blacks in the wartime defence projects, became a western city with a huge black population concentrated in a few ghetto areas just as in Chicago. And again, as in Chicago, this provided a large potential audience for blues music, which new record companies tried to tap.

It was this movement of population which created a new blues style. It is often called Texas urban blues, indicating that it was an adaptation of traditional Texas rural blues to an urban context in cities like Los Angeles. Here the singer/guitarist T. Bone Walker was one of the most important musicians. He was born in Texas in 1913 but moved to California in 1934, beginning to record there in Los Angeles in 1940. His music was very different from the 'downhome' Chicago city blues. He would sing in a much smoother, quieter and more relaxed manner:

'More of a ballad, that's the kind of blues I like to play,' he has said. He was well known for his incredible technique on guitar, which was highlighted by the showmanship in his stage act. He would often hold the guitar away from his body, playing it with one hand only. But, apart from this, his manner of playing was different from the Delta blues style. Before, the guitarist usually played a number of notes at a time to produce chords, which were used to accompany the voice. But T. Bone developed a solo style, playing one string at a time to give a continuous series of notes to form a melody. In this he had been influenced by jazz guitarists who used a similar technique. It had been a jazz guitarist, Eddie Durham playing in Count Basie's Orchestra, who had first used the electric guitar. But T. Bone Walker became the first blues musician to do so. The electric guitar suited his style best because he could hit a single note and allow the amplified sound to continue for some time in order to build up musical tension and excitement. Many of T. Bone's records show another important aspect of the Texas urban blues style – the use of large groups featuring saxophones and brass as a background to the singer/guitarist. This was because the Kansas City blues style (discussed in chapter 5), as well as Texas rural blues, contributed to the new sound to produce a more jazz-based form of post-war urban blues.

It was Memphis, however, that was eventually to become the most important city in post-war blues. Situated about half-way between New Orleans and Chicago, this city had always been an important blues centre. In the 1920s it had been the home of the famous Memphis jug bands. These were groups featuring country blues singers backed by

opposite Record company release sheet for the Memphis Jug Band

MEMPHIS JUG BAND

V-38586 { **I Can Beat You Plenty** / Tired Of You Driving Me

V-38551 { **I Can't Stand It** / What's the Matter?

V-38578 { **I Whipped My Woman With a Single Tree** / Feed Your Friend With A Long-Handled Spoon

V-38558 { **K. C. Moan** / Memphis Yo Ho Blues

20552 { **Stingy Woman—Blues** / Sun Brimmers   Blues

V-38537 { **Mississippi River Waltz** / Jug Band Waltz

V-38504 { **Whitewash Station Blues** / Stealin,' Stealin'

✈ V-38015 { **A Black Woman Is Like a Black Snake** / On the Road Again

21185 { **Kansas City Blues** / State of Tennessee Blues

20576 { **Memphis Jug—Blues** / Newport News—Blues

Victor Division · RCA Victor Company, Inc.
Camden   New Jersey

instruments like fiddles, banjos, washboards and jugs. The 'jug' was simply a bottle over which the musician blew at different angles to add a booming bass sound rather like a tuba. These groups by no means always played blues; they were simply entertainment bands playing at dances, picnics and so on.

The growth of Memphis as a key blues centre after the Second World War was largely due to the influence of radio, together with the recording industry. From 1948 onwards, the WDIA (a black-owned radio station in Memphis) directed its programmes at an exclusively black audience. For twenty hours a day and seven days a week, a continuous programme of blues and gospel music records, together with some live shows, was played

A radio station disc jockey

to a potential audience of 1.25 million black people.

For a couple of years in the late 1940s, a young black disc jockey had played the records of his choice on this station. He had a variety of tastes – born in Mississippi, he liked the Delta blues style. But he also loved the records of the Texas urban blues musicians. As a guitarist himself, he was keen to listen to as many styles as possible, so that he could play in a way which took the best of all of them. This he did and soon he was to be recognised as the greatest figure in post-war blues. His name was B. B. 'Blues Boy' King.

B. B. King   Few people would now dispute B. B. King's title of 'King of the Blues'. In cities like Chicago he can still pack the largest theatres with an audience of black people, at a time when, as we shall be seeing later, soul has largely replaced blues as the music of the ghetto. At the same time, his influence on rock guitarists has given him a large, white audience capable of packing concert halls in England, as well as in the USA.

He made his first record in 1949 and by the early 1950s was making hit after hit. The earliest music he had heard was that of both Delta and Texas rural blues. But he still remembers the first impact of T. Bone Walker's playing: 'That was the first electric guitar I'd ever heard . . . and I went crazy, I went completely nutty. . . . I think that he had the clearest touch of anybody I'd ever heard on guitar then.' Working later as a disc jockey he could listen to other brands of black music as well – gospel music and the jazz guitar of players like Charlie Christian and even the famous French gypsy jazz guitarist, Django Reinhardt.

Given his sort of background, it's perhaps not

surprising that B. B. King should have created a new urban blues style which reflected a wide variety of influences. His vocals were relaxed, but delivered in a manner suggestive of the call-and-response pattern of gospel singing. Instead of singing aggressively on the beat, he would use a subtle behind-the-beat phrasing, creating the kind of swing feel that a jazz vocalist aims for. His guitar style was partly jazz-influenced, with solos based on fast single-note runs in the manner of T. Bone. His bands usually consisted of eight or nine musicians. There was no harmonica, as in the Chicago 'downhome' style, but instead saxophones and brass instruments played as arranged backings to the vocals and guitar solos.

Now over fifty, B. B. King is still going strong. His concerts are emotional events, usually beginning with an instrumental number. Then, lowering the volume, he introduces the members of his band, ending with 'and, of course, this is Lucille' – a reference to his guitar. He's called his guitar that ever since a night he was playing in a small dance hall near Memphis. Two men got into a fight over a woman, knocked over a kerosene heater, and the place burnt to the ground. The only thing B. B. King rescued was his guitar, which he promptly named after the woman who had caused the fight – Lucille. Following the band introductions, B. B. King says something like: 'We're going to try and move you tonight. If you like the blues, I think we can,' and then he goes immediately into a piercing guitar solo, screwing his face up almost as if he's in pain. In fact this is just an expression of the emotional way he plays. Not only can his long, wailing, bending guitar notes have an incredible effect on his audience, but he has also been known to move himself to tears by his own music. And, just like all the greatest blues singers,

B. B. King

when he sings, he sings about common troubles and refers to situations that will have affected most of his black audience. The audience will yell back phrases to show their agreement with the message of the song: his vocal lines being punctuated by 'yea, yea' or 'say it again'. And B. B. King himself will talk back: 'thank you', 'thank you' he'll say, after receiving rapturous applause for one of his guitar solos in the middle of a number. Such performer/ audience interplay is an important part of all live blues performances, and goes back to the traditional black call-and-response pattern, as well as the song-sermons mentioned in chapter 2.

B. B. King is a brilliant guitarist and a superb

vocalist as well. But the history of the blues shows how many fine musicians (like Robert Johnson and Little Walter) came to an early disastrous end through drink, drugs and other problems. B. B. King has never had such problems, although his marriage did break up as a result of his great dedication to his music. He is a real professional and has reached his undisputed 'King of the Blues' position not only by his great talent but through sheer hard work. The only life he knows is one of constant travel with his band from show to show. 'My home is usually a hotel room,' he said only a few years ago. 'My manager is up in New York and my mother and father are on a farm that I own with them outside Memphis. But me? Well I don't have a home, not really – I've got 300 working days this year, and recording dates on top of that. Where would I live?'

The decline of the blues

The B. B. King sound, together with that of other blues musicians such as Bobby Bland and Junior Parker (who had also begun their recording careers in Memphis), soon became *the* modern urban blues sound. By the late 1950s, even Chicago, centre of the downhome city blues of artists like Muddy Waters, had given way to this newer sound. Numerous younger Chicago musicians, like Buddy Guy and Otis Rush, had taken B. B. King as their idol. This was all part of a rejection by the younger black audience of the more traditional sounding blues. The old Delta blues style, even when amplified to give a more powerful sound, seemed to hark back to the post-slavery days of the cotton fields of the south – an era that younger blacks wanted to forget. They associated it with the black lower class, with poor, uneducated rural workers who had only just come up from the south. To young blacks, born

opposite Poster
advertisement

BATTLE FOR THE KING OF THE BLUES
—AT—
THE AMPHITHEATRE
43rd AND HALSTED
FRI. - NOV. 7
ONE PERFORMANCE - 8:00 P.M.
★ ★ IN PERSON ★ ★

B. B. KING

PLUS

BOBBY BLAND
ALBERT KING - BENNY
LATIMORE - O. V. WRIGHT
THE HOWLING WOLF
JOHN LEE HOOKER
JIMMY REED - LITTLE MILTON
PLUS OTHER STARS

Tickets on Sale at All Ticketron Outlets, All Sears & Wards Stores
The Sugar Shack, 5525 South State
FOR INFORMATION CALL 684-3020

and brought up in Chicago, the newer, more modern
style of the Memphis sound was more appropriate.
Thus a typical fan's comment was: 'B. B.'s cleaned
up the blues; they've refined it, so it's smooth and
easy – no harps, moaning or shit like that. Those
guys have brought the blues up to date – made it
modern.'

But by the 1960s even the 'cleaner' urban blues
musicians were losing their audiences. Many record
companies had cut back on their blues recordings
after 1956 when, with the birth of rock 'n' roll, a new
potential mass market of white teenagers was
opened up. Younger blacks, on the other hand, had
created a demand for soul music. This, as will be
seen in the next chapter, was a more aggressive
form of black music that emerged out of a mixture of
blues, gospel music and jazz. Soul music was better
suited to a philosophy of black pride and a positive
fight against racial discontent – 'Say it loud, I'm
black and I'm proud,' sang soul singer James
Brown. The philosophy of the blues, on the other
hand, had always been one of having to accept a
bad situation and making the best of it.

Today, the main audience for the few remaining
black bluesmen is a white one – an audience
created by the interest of so many rock musicians in
blues music. In Chicago, of the old 'downhome' city
blues musicians, only Muddy Waters still has a
significant popularity among blacks (his big rival,
Howlin' Wolf, whose bands played in a similar style,
died in 1976). The modern urban blues musicians
like B. B. King are more popular with a black
audience, but have nevertheless often had to vary
their styles. B. B. King still remembers bitterly the
night a black audience booed him for playing straight
blues:

It really hurt in a way. I think maybe they're
ashamed of the blues. They think it's some kind
of old-fashioned Uncle Tom music. Well it's not.
It's the best music there is. And I got mad and told
them so.

Conclusion   After the Second World War there was a growth of
new blues styles, aided by rapid developments in
both the record industry and in radio networks
throughout the USA. The new styles reflected the
different paths that migrating blacks took. Since
Chicago became the home of so many rural workers
from the Mississippi area, it also became the home
of an electrically amplified city version of the old
Delta blues. In most other areas, and particularly in
Memphis, on the west coast and later in Chicago
itself, the urban blues sound (a mixture of many
previous styles) became the most popular. Other
cities also developed a distinctive sound. In New
Orleans, for example, Fats Domino and his band
were playing a music far removed from the country
blues, but rooted more in a jazz style, featuring
pianists and saxophonists.

The early 1950s were the boom years for the
modern urban and city blues music. But later, the
record industry and radio networks that had been
responsible for its growth, helped cause its decline
by shifting towards the kind of music popular with
the up-and-coming, white, teenage market. However,
while the blues as the living form of music for most
black people disappeared, its spirit lived on in the
new styles of soul music. At the same time, blues
became one of the main influences on contemporary
rock music and in the process captured a large
white audience for the first time. It is to such recent
developments that we turn our attention next.

8 The strands meet

Introduction   The main concern of this book to date has been to tell the story of blues and jazz from their earliest beginnings. Since the music was created by black Americans, it is to such musicians with their black audiences that most attention has been paid. However, one of the most significant aspects of this music is the way it has changed the course of modern popular music. Rock 'n' roll, rock, soul and Motown have all been developments from this black music tradition. How this all came about is the theme of this chapter.

Rhythm and blues or r and b   Between the two world wars, the records by black artists designed for a black audience were known as 'race' records. After the Second World War some major record companies, embarrassed by the associations of 'race', gave up this term and substituted rhythm and blues (r and b). By the early 1950s, this had become the generally accepted label for all black music intended for a black audience. As such, it included not only just blues music, but also gospel, ballads and the black vocal harmony sound of groups such as the Inkspots, the Platters and the Drifters.

As a label, r and b was a convenient one because one of the main characteristics of post-war blues was the addition of a strong rhythmic element with heavy backbeat drumming. The downhome Chicago city blues and the urban blues of musicians like B. B. King were both an important part of the r and b record market. Another major influence came from the big swing jazz bands of the 1930s, especially the more blues-based ones. With the rise of bebop jazz, many big band musicians were worried that the new music would no longer appeal to such a wide audience since people couldn't dance to it. Louis Jordan, for example, who had played in bands featuring the great jazzmen Charlie Parker and Dizzy Gillespie, decided that 'those guys . . . really wanted to play mostly for themselves, and I still wanted to play for the people. I just like to sing my blues and swing.' So, in 1938, Louis formed his own group called the Tympany Five. They played a mixture of r and b and jazz with Louis himself both singing and playing alto saxophone. Called 'jump' blues, this style was based on the jumpy nature of boogie-woogie piano rhythms. Louis's band was very popular in the 1940s, not only with black audiences but with white ones too. As well as his entertaining stage act and use of witty lyrics, Louis sang in a very clear voice which was more easily understood by whites than the blacker sound of most other blues singers. Perhaps this is why, as a style, it was later to have a big impact on white singers like Bill Haley who introduced rock 'n' roll.

With bands like Count Basie's in the 1930s, big band jazz and blues had been almost inseparable. The arrival of bop brought a split between jazz and blues. The more complicated rhythms and harmonies of bop meant that the music lost touch with the majority of the black audience. But the big band blues tradition continued in the form of r and b. It differed from jazz in having a regular, swinging, danceable rhythm, and was presented in an entertaining way, with a great deal of showmanship. Saxophone soloists, in particular, would create a stir by playing on their knees, bending over backwards with their saxes up in the air. Musical tension and excitement would be generated by a combination of the whole band playing riffs, or repeated phrases, and the tenor sax blasting through this background in a solo.

The blues shouter Joe Turner came from a musical tradition like this. Born in Kansas City, he had often jammed with musicians from the Count Basie Band. But he always had a stronger, harsher, more bluesy voice than Basie's main vocalist, Jimmy Rushing, who leaned closer to a jazz feel. In the late 1930s, Turner went to New York and teamed up with the boogie pianist Pete Johnson. In 1939, they made the best-selling 'Roll 'Em Pete' record, a lively, driving sound although using only piano and vocals. After the Second World War they played together again, but this time with a full band using a rhythm section and trumpet and sax soloists. Then electric guitars were added and, by the early 1950s, this particular style of r and b had come closest to the new, and this time white, musical revolution – the sound of rock 'n' roll.

From r and b to rock 'n' roll and soul

In the early 1950s, the popular music world was clearly split between a white side and a black side. Whites listened to white ballad 'crooners' like Johnny Ray and Doris Day who sang Tin Pan Alley popular songs. Blacks had their own music in r and b (although sometimes, as with the 'doo-wop' black vocal harmony groups, this was Tin Pan Alley music, but adapted to be sung in a black music style).

There was a white hit parade and a black hit parade; white radio stations and black ones too. But at the same time an extraordinary thing was happening. Owners of record stores found white youngsters buying the black r and b records, and even dancing madly to them in the record shops. At home they would tune in their radios to the sound of the black stations, not the white. This happened particularly in those areas, like Memphis and Mississippi, where the influence of the black radio stations was very strong. These white kids had found in r and b a raw excitement, and Tin Pan Alley now seemed wishy-washy in comparison. Soon a white disc jockey called Alan Freed started a white radio programme featuring r and b. He finally called it 'Rock and Roll Party', probably because so many of the r and b lyrics talked of 'rockin' ánd 'rollin', which were both references to sex. The response to his programme was fantastic. While some of the older generation called him a 'dirty nigger lover', disgusted at the way he was playing black music on white radio, the younger generation loved it. It was not long before Freed was promoting concerts by some of the great r and b artists for a white teenage audience, instead of their usual black one.

However, to be really successful with a large, white audience r and b had to be toned down a bit. In many cases the lyrics were *too* suggestive, the blues elements *too* strong. So, for the pop market, white performers provided their own versions, copying the r and b recordings in a manner more suited to a white audience. Thus Georgia Gibbs took her version of a number-one song from the r and b charts, Hank Ballard and the Midnighters' 'Work with me, Annie', almost to the top of the pop charts some months later. But, at that time, Ballard's lyrics were

NOTICE!

STOP

Help Save The Youth of America
DON'T BUY NEGRO RECORDS

(If you don't want to serve negroes in your place of business, then do not have negro records on your juke box or listen to negro records on the radio.)

The screaming, idiotic words, and savage music of these records are undermining the morals of our white youth in America.

Call the advertisers of the radio stations that play this type of music and complain to them!

Don't Let Your Children Buy, or Listen To These Negro Records

For additional copies of this circular, write
CITIZENS' COUNCIL OF GREATER NEW ORLEANS, INC.
509 Delta Building   New Orleans Louisiana 70112

Permission is granted to re-print this circular

too vulgar, with the obvious sexual meaning attached
to the word 'work':

Work with me, Annie
Let's get it while the gitting is good.

So in Gibbs's version even the title had to be
changed. 'Work' became 'dance' and the lyrics now
ran:

Dance with me, Henry
Let's dance while the music rolls on.

Rock 'n' roll's takeover of the pop music industry
from the mid-1950s onwards is covered in detail by
Dave Rogers in *Rock 'n' Roll*. The black elements of
r and b were merged with white influences like
country and western music, and soon there were
white idols such as Elvis Presley. Songs based on
early blues or later r and b records designed only for
a black audience, became big hits when sung by
Presley. Even some black artists made the change
to performing rock 'n' roll for a white audience. For
example, in 1955 Chuck Berry moved from St Louis,
where he was playing guitar in a trio at night clubs,
to Chicago. As soon as he arrived he made a tour of
the new city's jazz and blues clubs and ended up
asking Muddy Waters if he could play a number with
his group. Muddy was so impressed that he referred
Berry to Leonard Chess, president of Chess
Records, who, hearing some tapes, signed up
Chuck on the spot. Berry's first record, 'Maybelline',
soon became the most popular record on Alan
Freed's radio rock 'n' roll programme in New York.
Shortly afterwards, his 'Roll Over Beethoven', later to
be a hit for the Beatles, went in to the American hit
parade. Chuck Berry was set on the road to
becoming the future black king of rock 'n' roll.

Other black r and b artists like Fats Domino, playing a kind of 'jump' blues in New Orleans, also made it big in the white rock 'n' roll market. But for most black musicians the change in their style required for success was too great. Much of Chuck Berry's impact was due to the way his lyrics were directed at a white, teenage audience – rebellious songs against school, work and parents. He sang of a life of excitement and fun; his lyrics talked of fast cars, dancing and teenage emotions of sex and first love. Most r and b artists couldn't or didn't want to do this. The experiences they sang of were common to black, not white, people and their whole approach was too raw for a white audience.

However, changes were taking place in black r and b as well. Ray Charles had begun to learn the piano on entering a blind school, after a disease had left him incurably blind at the age of six. In the mid-1950s he stopped singing his traditional twelve-bar blues numbers and experimented by recording a traditional gospel song instead. The resulting 'I Got a Woman' was a pure mixture of blues and gospel. The piano became the dominant instrument instead of the guitar of his earlier blues recordings. A brass and sax section played in call-and-response fashion, like a traditional gospel music chorus, to build up the musical excitement. And through it all came the bluesy voice of Charles himself, using also the gospel singer's techniques of repetition and shouts for emotional effect. Many older black people were horrified. Rarely before had religious music, like gospel singing, been mixed with blues. Indeed, for the religious, blues had often been seen as the devil's music, since many of its traditional themes, like sex, were seen as sinful. Mahalia Jackson, the most famous modern singer of black church gospel

opposite Chuck Berry

music, always refused to sing blues numbers. But even some traditional blues musicians were upset by Ray Charles's singing. Big Bill Broonzy's verdict was, 'He's mixin' the blues with the spirituals . . . I know that's wrong. . . . He's got a good voice but it's a church voice. He should be singin' in a church.'

However, almost singlehanded, Ray Charles had created the black music of the future – soul music. Other musicians joined blues and gospel. Charles himself played in some jazz groups, which led to jazz musicians like the saxophonist Cannonball Adderley blending jazz, gospel and blues to give a type of hard-bop 'soul jazz'. Such an influence spread to other famous jazz musicians like the band leader and composer Charlie Mingus whose groups produced some of the most powerful and emotionally based jazz of the post-war period.

By the mid-1960s soul music had become the main form of black popular music. But more than this, through artists like the Supremes on the famous Tamla Motown recording label and Otis Redding and Wilson Pickett on the famous Stax and Atlantic labels, this new music became truly international in scope. Today the British hit parade continues to have its share of soul and Motown records in it, and soul stars like James Brown and Aretha Franklin are heard throughout the world. So important has been this particular development from r and b that another book in this series is devoted to examining it in detail – Simon Frith's *Soul and Motown*.

The blues boom in England

The earliest widespread interest in blues in England came through jazz. Following the Second World War, a small group of enthusiasts in England were playing what was called 'revivalist' jazz. This movement, both in the USA and Europe, was associated with musicians who rejected the new bop jazz developments of the 1940s, preferring to recreate the sound of traditional New Orleans-type jazz. Such traditional jazz would probably have remained the music of an enthusiastic few, played in the top rooms of pubs and in small clubs, had it not been for a banjo player called Lonnie Donegan. He played in Ken Colyer's traditional jazz band in the early 1950s, but in between jazz sets Colyer encouraged Donegan to change over to guitar and sing some old American blues numbers. Then when trombonist Chris Barber left Colyer to form his own trad jazz band, he took Donegan with him. The interval sets

Ken Colyer's
Jazz Men

continued but with Donegan backed by Chris Barber
playing bass and the band's singer, Beryl Bryden,
playing a washboard with thimbles on her fingers. It
was this little trio that recorded the famous 'Rock
Island Line', which, when it was released as a single,
remained in the British Top Twenty for seventeen
weeks, and eventually sold nearly 2 million copies.

Lonnie Donegan had launched a new craze –
skiffle. Based on early blues and Memphis jug-band
music, the big attraction of skiffle was that it was a
'homemade' music. Thousands of youngsters formed
skiffle groups by making their own instruments to
accompany the guitar, just as the earliest black
blues singers had done. Double-basses were simply
an old tea chest with a broom handle fixed to one
corner and a piece of string stretched from the top of
the handle to the opposite corner of the chest! The
skiffle boom soon ended, but its influence was
enormous. It had encouraged thousands of
youngsters to learn the guitar by copying the chords
of Donegan's simple, catchy songs. This is the way
John Lennon and Paul McCartney of the Beatles
began. John's first band, the Quarrymen, was a
skiffle group, complete with tea-chest bass. Skiffle
had also introduced a great many teenagers to the
music of black Americans. Many of Lonnie
Donegan's songs had come from a black country
folk-blues singer called Huddie Ledbetter.
Nicknamed Leadbelly, he had been discovered on a
prison farm in the southern states of America, where
he was serving a sentence for murder. His obvious
talent as a blues singer and twelve-string guitarist
was recognised by the folk and blues researcher,
John Lomax, who later brought about Leadbelly's
release. The old country blues and work songs
Leadbelly played had gone out of fashion for black

audiences in the 1940s. His folk-blues style, however, was popular with those whites who were becoming increasingly interested in jazz and blues. This applied particularly in Europe, which Leadbelly managed to visit just before his death in 1949.

The seeds of a widespread interest in American blues had been sown in Britain. They came to flower in the British r and b boom of the early 1960s. Many groups, particularly in London, began playing blues music based on the Chicago City 'downhome' style. R and b clubs sprouted up, in many cases taking over previous trad jazz clubs. The Rolling Stones took their name from an early Muddy Waters record, 'Rollin' Stone' and featured another Waters record 'I Just Wanna Make Love To You' on their first LP. Soon many of the best pop groups of the mid-1960s, like the Beatles, the Animals and the Who, were playing material first recorded by black American musicians. The blues had crossed the Atlantic and had become the foundation of the British pop music boom.

The blues revival

The early English r and b groups were followed in the late 1960s by a host of rock stars whose music was also rooted in the blues. It was a group called John Mayall's Bluesbreakers which formed the bridge between the early English r and b and the later blues-based rock. Mayall marked the beginning of an age when the spotlight in a rock band was placed firmly on the lead guitarist. Many guitarists who once played in his group went on to star in others afterwards – Peter Green to the group Fleetwood Mac, Mick Taylor to the Rolling Stones. But the most famous of Mayall's ex-guitarists was Eric Clapton, whose story is a familiar one:

At first I played exactly like Chuck Berry for six or seven months . . . then I got into older bluesmen. Because he was so readily available I dug Big Bill Broonzy; then I heard a lot of cats I had never heard of before like Robert Johnson. Later I turned on to B. B. King and it's been that way ever since. I still don't think there has ever been a better blues guitarist in the world than B. B. King.

Groups like Cream, with Clapton on lead guitar, and the Jimi Hendrix Experience, played a loud, amplified form of blues music. Hendrix, in particular, stretched the electric guitar to its outer limits using deliberate distortion and feedback for musical effect. The other major influence from black r and b, apart from the dominance of the electric guitar, was the vocal tone singers used. John Lennon of the Beatles said it all when he jokingly boasted that 'we sing more coloured than the Africans.' In this respect soul music was a vital factor. Many famous rock singers from Mick Jagger of the Rolling Stones to Roger Daltry of the Who have acknowledged their debt to great soul artists like Ray Charles and Otis Redding.

So English rock music in the 1960s had its roots firmly in black American music – in urban and city blues, r and b, soul and Motown. But, funnily enough, this was not the music that at that time had a big appeal for much white youth in the USA. They were caught up in a folk music and social protest movement, featuring singer/guitarists like Bob Dylan and Joan Baez. For those interested in folk music, if they had any interest in blues at all, it was in the older country blues styles, not in the urban electric blues. So, although many whites had continued to listen to black music on the radio, when English groups like the Beatles and the Rolling Stones first toured the USA in the early 1960s, some Americans hardly knew what had hit them. But whatever it was, they liked it and before long musicians were putting aside their folk music acoustic guitars and taking up electric ones instead. For many white school and college students, hearing the Rolling Stones was the first time they had heard the electric blues, despite the fact that the music had originated in their own country.

Thus an interest in blues by English rock musicians led to a massive blues revival in the USA. While black audiences were turning their back on the blues as an outdated music, whites turned to it for the basis of their rock music. In the process they provided a huge new audience for the great black blues musicians. John Lee Hooker was one such musician who took on a new lease of life:

> It may seem corny to you, but this is true: the groups from England really started the blues rolling and getting bigger among the kids – the white kids. At one time the blues was just among the blacks – the older black people. And this uprise started in England by the Beatles, Animals, Rolling Stones, it started everybody to digging the blues. It got real big over there, and then people in the States started to catch on. The last eight or ten years, I really been making it big.

Most of the top urban and city blues musicians now play mainly to white audiences. Some of them have actually played and toured with white groups. John Lee Hooker recorded a brilliant album 'Hooker 'n' Heat' with the white, American blues band Canned Heat. He has also toured with the Rolling Stones. Muddy Waters, also, has recorded with some of the best-known white American blues

Son House

musicians, including the Paul Butterfield Blues Band and Johnny Winter.

The blues revival didn't affect just the post-war urban and city blues musicians. White blues enthusiasts travelled to the deep south of the USA to try and find some of the older country blues musicians who had not been heard of for a long time. Their interest had been stimulated partly by rock music, but also by many American folk musicians singing in the older blues styles. The famous folk singer Bob Dylan, for example, included mostly blues songs on his first album. The blues researchers' work not only led to a vastly increased knowledge of the history of the blues, but to the 'rediscovery' of older musicians, who were persuaded to pick up their guitars again and play to a new, white audience in folk blues festivals. Son House, for example, had played both with Charley Patton and Robert Johnson. But he had given up playing altogether, after being discouraged by the changing trends in blues away from his solo Delta blues style. It was on 23 June 1964 that three white blues researchers, who had spent months trying to find Son House, finally made it to his home in Rochester, New York, after travels that had taken them through sixteen states. At first, House, who was then sixty-two years old, couldn't believe that some of the records he'd made so long ago had become very popular in both Europe and the USA. Although he was frightened by the prospect of performing again, he was soon persuaded: 'I just didn't think that anyone was interested in that old-time stuff any more. Couldn't understand why some white boys were so interested but I agreed to try again.' Soon he was launched on a new career, which included recording and touring Britain as well as the USA. The blues he played was exactly the same as what he had played forty years before. But instead of an audience of fellow black farmworkers, he was entertaining audiences of thousands of white people, many of whom had never been to the USA, let alone Mississippi.

Jazz today   Interest in the blues has thus been revived by recent developments in pop music. But rock music has also played a part in increasing the appreciation of jazz as well. This has resulted from the merging of the two styles of music into jazz-rock. The trumpeter Miles Davis was the first jazz musician to make serious experiments using rock music effects. He introduced to jazz the use of electric instruments, where before the guitar and organ had been the only ones to be amplified electrically. In came the electric bass, electric piano and even fuzz boxes and wah-wah pedals for Miles's trumpet – extra effects that in rock were usually used only for the lead guitar. This all made the music sound very different from previous jazz. The feel was different too – moving away from a swing-type jazz rhythm to the more rocking feel of a rock band.

Many conventional jazz musicians wrote off Miles's rock influences as simply an attempt to make his music more commercial. This seems unlikely in view of the way that Miles himself has always been at the head of new developments in jazz. Whatever his motives, Miles's music has had an enormous impact on the music of the 1970s. A number of musicians beginning in Miles's groups have gone on to lead their own bands playing an electrically amplified, rock-flavoured style of jazz. Electric pianist Joe Zawinul and sax player Wayne Shorter left Miles to form the influential jazz-rock group 'Weather Report'

Miles Davis in concert at a Berlin jazz festival

in 1970. The British guitarist John McLaughlin, after playing on Miles's famous 'In a Silent Way' recording of 1969, went on to play in other groups like 'Lifetime' and the 'Mahavishnu Orchestra', which also included a number of English rock musicians.

All this has led many rock musicians to a greater interest in jazz. The more adventurous rock bands, particularly in the late 1960s in the USA had always been conscious of jazz influences – saxophonist John Coltrane, in particular, was often singled out as a favourite. But recently the jazz-rock developments have meant that many more conventional rock groups have added sax players. They were used either to give a punchy musical background to the sound or even to add solos in a jazz style.

However, jazz-rock is by no means the only important new jazz style. The American jazz free-form approach we looked at in chapter 6 is paralleled in Europe by equally strong movements. In England there is a small group of musicians influenced both by free-form jazz developments and by avant-garde, European classical music. Musicians such as guitarist Derek Bailey, saxophonist Evan Parker and drummer John Stevens play an experimental style of 'free music'. As with many adventurous innovators, their audience is a relatively small one, but their influence on numerous other English musicians has been considerable.

A common feature of recent jazz developments in both Europe and the USA is the attempt by musicians to increase the control over the promotion and recording of their own music. For years many of the greatest black jazz musicians were exploited by white-owned jazz clubs and record companies, whose primary interest has usually been commercial profit rather than the making of good music. Annoyed by the way record companies had rejected their material as 'not commercial', free-form musicians have now set up their own organisations and record labels. Thus, for the first time in the USA, black Americans were able to take control of their own music. And as well as playing in the normal jazz clubs, many of the country's best jazz musicians have played regularly in lofts and warehouses in a small section of New York City. This way they could play the way they wanted to, unhindered by club owners, who are more concerned with their bar profits than with the music. Instead, a growing audience of jazz lovers paid only a small admission fee to the warehouses, brought their own food and drink and listened to the musicians' jam sessions for as long as they liked.

Between the extremes of jazz-rock and free form lie a host of jazz musicians playing in more conventional styles – traditional and modern. Jazz has become an international music played and loved all over the world. But perhaps because of its origins

in the music of ex-slaves, it has often been seen as
a kind of unconventional, protest music. In the USA,
the country of its birth, jazz has never received the
status and prestige it deserves, mainly because of a
white society's unwillingness to recognise black
people's achievements. When Duke Ellington, one of
the greatest musicians the USA has ever produced,
was turned down for an annual Pulitzer Prize for
music in 1965, he commented:

> I'm hardly surprised that my kind of music is still
> without, let us say, official honour at home. Most
> Americans still take it for granted that Europe-
> based music – classical music, if you will – is the
> only really respectable kind.

Consequently the musical achievements of jazz
musicians have often been more readily recognised
in Europe than in the USA. But even in England, jazz
has always had a raw deal. While classical music
receives extensive economic support from the
government, jazz has only recently started receiving
subsidies, and then only very small ones. More
important, the BBC's radio policy of promoting
classical music on Radio 3, light music on Radio 2
and commercial pop on Radio 1, means that jazz
hardly gets a look in. Some of our top jazz
musicians, like baritone sax player John Surman,
have often been voted in international polls the best
musicians in the world on their instruments. Yet
British jazz musicians find it far easier to give radio
concerts in Germany, Sweden, Holland and other
European countries than in their own home country!
Thus jazz trumpeter Ian Carr has sadly commented
that, 'the enlightened German radio, for instance,
unlike our own, divides its music into three
categories: light entertainment, serious – and jazz.'

Conclusion

Much of this chapter has been concerned with the ways in which traditional barriers within black music have been breaking down. Some of the best music around today is hard to pigeonhole as either jazz, soul or rock. We are no longer surprised to find musicians naming as their main influences black people as varied as Ornette Coleman, Chuck Berry, James Brown, Stevie Wonder and Miles Davis. However different these musicians may sound on record, it is now widely recognised that they are all part of a continuing black music tradition. And the influence of this tradition is to be found all over the world. Films increasingly use black music soundtracks, particularly 'crossover' jazz (as mixtures of jazz and rock have come to be called). But, above all, the impact of the black music tradition is to be found in the wide variety of pop music styles, which have become truly international in scope.

above The jazz-rock group Nucleus, led by Ian Carr

9 Conclusion

This book has been about the development of a new musical tradition. It is often called Afro-American music, indicating its influences from both Africa and the USA. Beginning as the music of a suppressed group of black ex-slaves, we have seen how it has had an enormous impact on the music of the Western world. Many people have suggested that, because of its interest in rhythm and in making instruments imitate the voice, Afro-American music has revitalised the Western musical tradition – in a more positive way than has any other musical style during the twentieth century.

The blues began as a vocal music, with its origins deep in the heart of the work songs and field hollers of the black man's slavery days. The most important aspect of the blues music tradition is that it has been an oral rather than a notated one. Singers and musicians learn by listening to others. When they play, they improvise rather than read music from a musical score. As blues musician Mance Lipscomb has put it:

> I been playing the git-tar now 'bout forty-nine years and then I started out by myself, just heard it and learned it. Ear music. And nobody didn't learn me nothin'. Just pick it up myself; I didn't know any notes, just play by ear.

The spontaneity of the blues

The musicians play in subtle rhythms, whose basis lies in African music. They bend notes on their instruments, leading to emotionally expressive wailing and whining effects. To achieve this they sometimes use special attachments like the bottleneck on the guitar. They sing in tones of voice far removed from that of the traditional European vocalist. Consequently the music does not sound like traditional classical music.

European writers and musicians have often failed to recognise the importance of the lack of musical notation in blues music. Musical notation can indicate the fixed pitches and precisely measured rhythmic durations that are essential to classical music, but it cannot convey the bent pitches, variety of tone and degrees of rhythmic accentuation which are at the heart of the blues. Thus W. C. Handy is often referred to as the 'Father of the Blues' because he composed famous tunes like 'St. Louis Blues' as early as 1914. But Handy, while certainly popularising blues by composing and writing them down to be played (usually by jazz musicians), distorted the nature of true blues in the process. What does a *real* blues musician think of 'St. Louis Blues'? 'That's a pretty tune and it has kind of a bluesy tone, but that's not the blues. You can't dress up the blues. I'm not saying that St. Louis Blues isn't fine music, you understand. But it just isn't blues,' said T. Bone Walker. It is the importance of learning blues music by ear which explains why the famous singer Alberta Hunter can say: 'As for musicians who could play the blues. Well the ones that didn't know music could play the best blues. I know that I don't want no musicians who know all about music playin' for me.'

But the situation with jazz was quite different.

Partly because of the influence of the relatively well-educated Creoles in New Orleans, jazz was affected much more by European music than was blues. While many of the earliest jazz musicians couldn't read music, as jazz progressed and became more complex, it became more necessary to have some knowledge of traditional music notation. But jazz has always kept the essential characteristics of the blues tradition. However sophisticated and musically advanced, jazz has continually retained the special Afro-American rhythmic approach, as well as the freedom of expression learned in improvisation. It has also always used instruments in a very flexible way to copy the human voice, just as blues has done. A striking example of this is given by the great Creole saxophonist Sydney Bechet's advice to a pupil:

> I am going to give you one note today. See how many ways you can play that note – growl it, smear it, flat it, sharp it, do anything you want to it. That's how you express your feelings in music. It's like talking.

This is obviously rather different from the approach of the classical music instrumental teacher! But it explains why a fellow musician could describe even the complex, big-band orchestrations of Duke Ellington in the following way: 'He used the sound of the city in his writing, but whatever he does, you can always hear the blues.' The familiar twelve-bar blues form has also remained part of the language of all jazz styles, acting as a foundation on which musicians improvised. Many of the bop innovators in the 1940s took the blues as a basis on which to create new themes and melodies. Trumpeter Howard McGhee, talking of Charlie Parker's music, has said:

'Bird could make more tunes out of the blues than any musician who ever lived.'

In a short book like this we have only been able to pick out a few key individuals in the development of the Afro-American musical tradition. Similarly we have concentrated on a few major themes. One has been the spread of this new music in the USA as a result of black people's migrations, together with the influence of radio and records. Another theme has been how the music has always been deeply expressive of the attitudes of black people to an obviously prejudiced white society. In particular, the blues spirit of resignation has given way to a more aggressive black pride and 'soul solidarity' in recent years. Most important of all, perhaps, has been the continuing impact of Afro-American music on popular music.

Tin Pan Alley, the commercial American popular music industry, has always used watered-down elements of black music, from ragtime to bop harmonies, to spice up popular songs. In the 1930s jazz reached mass audiences in the Swing Era. Many jazz singers starting then, such as Ella Fitzgerald, went on to become increasingly popular as singers of traditional popular songs as well as jazz numbers. And then in the 1950s rhythm and blues provided the basis for rock 'n' roll and later developments in soul and rock music. Through all these changes, certain basic elements have remained present, notably the blues approach to music making, and the call-and-response patterns, which can be traced back through gospel music and spirituals to Africa. In England, this Afro-American music has recently merged with another black music tradition, that of the West Indies. This produces varieties of reggae and reggae-flavoured rock and soul music — music that is examined by Dick Hebdige in *Reggae and Caribbean Music.*

It is one of the great miracles of the twentieth century that a music with such humble beginnings should have the power to rise beyond them to a position of international appeal. An inevitable consequence has been that aspects of the original folk art of blues music have been lost. Those blues lyrics, whose references had such deep meaning for audiences of black communities in the deep south of America, have become meaningless strings of words in the hands of white rock musicians. But, despite this, much of the spirit of black American music has been retained. And whatever the fads and fashions in future popular music, it is this black spirit which will almost certainly remain.

Glossary of musical terms

Afro-American music Any music which combined African and European elements. Such music was originally made by black people in America, but the term can now be applied to any music in the style.

arrangement An *arranger* produces a version of an existing piece of music for performance by a particular combination of musicians (unlike a *composer*, who creates new pieces of music). In making an *arrangement* he may merely put it into suitable **notation**, add **harmony**, make an **orchestration**, or he may make considerable changes, so as to give the music his personal interpretation (as in, for example, the arrangements of Glenn Miller).

backbeat drumming Drumming in which the *backbeat* (also called the *offbeat*) is strongly stressed (i.e., one TWO three FOUR). This sound is very typical of r and b and rock 'n' roll.

ballad This word has several meanings. In this book it means: (1) A long folksong, telling a story which may be true or fictional. (For further details see *Folksong and Music Hall*, chapters 1 and 2.) From this meaning comes the term *black ballad*, which means a ballad produced by black American singers as a result of blending **Afro-American** approaches and the white folk ballad. (2) A short popular song, usually fairly slow, of the sort produced by Tin Pan Alley.

bar Most Western music has a basic beat (often known as the pulse) to which you can tap your foot or dance. This pulse usually runs in a repeated pattern of 'strong' (louder) beats and 'weak' (softer) beats; this is known as the metre. In **Afro-American music** the commonest pattern (or *metre*) is: ONE two three four/ONE two three four, etc. One count of four is known as a *bar*. Other counts, such as three or five, can be used. These are also known as bars.

baritone horn A form of wind instrument, similar to a tuba, but higher in pitch. It is used in brass, military and American high school bands.

bass The lowest-pitched part in a piece of music. *String bass (double bass)*: a stringed instrument used for playing bass parts. In appearance like a large, upright violin.

blue note Blues musicians use a **scale** different from that traditionally used by classical musicians. The notes which were different were therefore often thought to be strange, wrong, or out of tune. These notes became known as *blue notes*.

bottleneck guitar A form of blues and rock guitar playing in which the left hand does not press down the strings. Instead it slides a smooth object, such as the neck of a bottle, along the strings to make different pitches.

call-and-response form A method of music making in which a leader (possibly improvising) sings a line (the *call*), and is answered by a chorus (the *response*). The *call* and *response* are usually one line long each. This procedure is an important feature of African and **Afro-American music**. In the latter it occurs, for example, between vocals and guitar in the country blues, between different **sections** in big band swing, and between preacher and congregation in **spiritual** and **gospel** singing.

camp meetings Religious mass meetings of the nineteenth century, held in the open air, and popular among both black and white Americans. They were a method favoured by Baptist and Methodist missionaries, and were in some ways rather like a modern open-air pop festival.

chord The result of sounding three or more notes together.

chord progression (Also **chord sequence**.) A fixed pattern of chords, used to accompany a melody, and which is then taken as a framework for improvisation by jazz musicians.

classical music A form of music created in Europe, or under a strong European influence, and preserved in musical **notation**. It is normally intended for attentive listening, either in concerts, or in religious ceremonies. Classical pieces tend to be of some length, and the composer pays special attention to problems of musical form. Though there are many modern composers of 'classical' or 'serious' music, in this book the term refers to music created before 1900. *Note*: The term 'Classical music' (with a capital C) is being used correctly only when it is applied to a particular style of the second half of the eighteenth century.

classic blues Blues music created by black Americans in the cities between about 1920 and 1935, and including a strong jazz influence.

composition (1) Any piece of original music. (2) The act of planning or preparing a piece of *original* music (in contrast to **arrangement**).

concerto A musical composition which features a solo instrument together with an orchestra or band.

cornet An instrument similar to a trumpet, but with a softer **timbre**. It was popular in brass and military bands, and under the influence of the latter was adopted by many New Orleans jazz musicians.

counterpoint In a musical **composition**, the art of combining melodies with each other, or setting them against each other at the same time.

country and western music The music which was most popular with white people in the southern states of the USA after about 1920. (For further details see *Rock 'n' Roll*, chapter 3.)

Delta blues Blues music produced in the period between about 1900 and 1940 in the Mississippi Delta.

falsetto A method of singing which results in notes higher in pitch than the natural voice. For example, a man singing falsetto will sound much like a woman.

feedback The noise produced when microphones pick up the sound coming out of the loudspeakers and so 'recycle' it. This results in a continuous sound, which grows in volume and unpleasantness. This problem often arises when amplification equipment is incorrectly placed or adjusted – the resulting whining and howling can ruin the performance. However, some rock musicians of the 1960s, notably the guitarist Jimi Hendrix, learned how to control feedback, and then used it deliberately in creating their music.

folk music The popular music of one community. In practice, the music of rural societies of the past. Folk music was usually sung, and was passed on by ear. *Note*: Though to many people the term 'folk music' suggests white British and American folk music, the term can be applied to music of any part of the world. Thus we can speak of 'black American folk music', 'African folk music', or 'Jamaican folk music', provided that the music is of the type described above.

form   The design or shape of a piece of music. Form is described: (1) by breaking the music down into sections; (2) by indicating the main musical ideas (especially the tunes); and (3) by listing the order in which these ideas appear, and any relationships between them.

fugue   One of the most important ways of shaping compositions in **counterpoint**. The most famous composer of fugue was J. S. Bach.

gospel music   Black American religious music performed in concert conditions by touring performers (as distinct from the spontaneous music of black American religious services).

harmony   (1) The harmony (or harmonies) of a tune are the **chords** which accompany it. (2) When musicians study harmony, they study *the rules governing the use of chords*. (3) To 'harmonise' a tune is to fit harmonies to it. *Note*: When Louis Armstrong worked out a harmony on the bandstand, he played along with King Oliver's tune, using the same *rhythm*, but different *notes*, selected from the chords (see pp. 44–5).

head arrangement   An arrangement which is not written down, but worked out quickly by ear and memorised. It is usually simpler than a written arrangement.

holler   (*also* 'field holler') A single line *call* sung by a black American field worker, or by a young man as a form of 'signature tune'.

improvisation   This word has several meanings. In this book it means: (1) The act of composing music at the moment of performance, rather than planning it beforehand. (The word is used in this sense in relation to free jazz, see p. 89). (2) Music in which the artist has planned the basic structure of a piece, but leaves decisions about some aspects of expression, rhythm, etc. until the moment of performance. (The word is used in this sense in relation to much popular music, black and white, such as blues singing, soul music, and white dance music.) (3) (With reference to earlier styles of jazz.) The on-the-spot composition of new lines of music, or very free versions of the melody. Such improvisation takes place over a set **chord progression**.

intonation The production of a note by the voice or by an instrument. Often we speak of 'faulty intonation', meaning that a note is played or sung out of tune.

jam session An informal gathering of jazz musicians for the purpose of improvising music freely and at length.

key Most classical, popular and earlier jazz music is said to be in a *key*, for example, 'the key of C'. This means that a particular **scale**, and the chords which can be derived from it, are used. More important, one note will be of greater importance than all the others (the note after which the key is named). The whole piece of music will move towards this note, especially at the end.

lyric The words of a song.

melody (1) This means the same as 'tune'. (2) It can also mean the most prominent (and usually highest-pitched) part in a piece of music.

metre See **bar**.

mode A type of **scale**, different in effect to those traditionally used by European classical composers, Tin Pan Alley songwriters, and composers and improvisers of earlier styles of jazz. Miles Davis used modes to break away from the sound of earlier jazz (see p. 89).

mute An object placed in the bell of a brass instrument in order to alter the sound of the instrument.

notation This term can be used in several slightly different ways and can mean: (1) printed or written copies of pieces of music; (2) a system of writing down music; (3) the act of writing down music.

offbeat See **backbeat drumming**.

orchestration The aspect of **composition** or arranging which is concerned with decisions about the combination of the different instruments in an orchestra. *Note*: In popular music an *orchestration* is a version for a big band of an existing piece of music. In it, among other things, the arranger alters the instrumentation.

phrase Several notes which make up a very short tune. A single melodic idea.

phrasing The interpretation of a **phrase** (by playing louder/softer, shorter/longer, smoother/rougher, etc.) to give it expressiveness and meaning.

pitch The level of a note sounded (that is, whether it is 'high' or 'low'). Pitch can be described by scientists in terms of the number of times per second at which a source of sound (e.g. a guitar string) vibrates.

pocket trumpet A small trumpet, used originally to obtain high notes more easily.

popular music Any music which is liked by a very large number of people (a mass audience). Usually, but not always, the taste of the majority. Popular music is also often defined, in contrast to **classical music**, as music for which a special training is not needed. This is not strictly correct, but it is true to say that popular music is music which is not normally studied in the music education system (e.g. in music colleges).

pop music The music favoured by young people (under 25) since about 1955. The term includes rock 'n' roll, reggae, Tamla Motown, etc.

quadrille A social dance of the eighteenth and nineteenth centuries. The dance is in four-beat time, and consists of five musical sections. The dancers dance in sets of four couples each.

ragtime The first form of **Afro-American music** to become widely popular with white people (about 1895–1920). It was usually played on the piano, and used a range of characteristic rhythms derived from black American **folk music**. (For further details see: *Jazz and Blues*, pp. 22–4; *Tin Pan Alley*, chapter 3.)

riff A musical technique which consists of the repetition of a particular **phrase**. It is often used to build up excitement. The **sections** of swing bands played riffs for this purpose, in **call-and-response form**.

ring shout A form of black religious folk dance in which the dancers move round in a circle, singing at the same time.

rock A form of popular music which emerged in the 1960s, appealing mostly to white people. Its main sources of influence were rock 'n' roll, r and b, blues, and white American folk music.

scale A set of pitches, most commonly arranged in ascending order, out of which musical tunes or compositions are made.

section A group of musicians in a jazz big band, who all play the same instruments, and usually at the same time.

song-sermon A black American religious service in which the preacher delivers a sermon, and gradually breaks into song. This is replied to in **call-and-response form** by the congregation.

spiritual (Also previously known as 'Negro spiritual'.) A slow, tuneful, religious song created by black Americans.

strict tempo dancing Literally, this means 'dancing at a fixed speed'. The term is now an alternative for 'ballroom dancing' (that is, the type of dancing which features especially the quickstep, waltz, slow foxtrot and tango). The term arose in the 1920s, when dance teachers wished to impose greater order upon the variety of dances which then existed, and the speeds at which they were taken. A *strict tempo orchestra* played dances at the speeds which were considered correct by teachers of dancing.

suite A form of **composition**, based on types of dance. The term and the approach are used by both classical and jazz composers, though the types of dances used differ greatly.

syncopation (1) Strictly speaking, *syncopation* refers to a rhythmic stress that is deliberately misplaced. In syncopation, the stresses in one or more lines of the music are different from those of the basic pattern (or *metre* – see **bar**), and clash with them. (2) Especially with reference to earlier jazz, people often said that the music was 'syncopated'. By this they meant not only that an occasional note clashed with the basic *metre*, but that whole **phrases** did so. Also, such people were thinking of the fact that, unlike in most of the classical music they knew, jazz used this type of rhythmic effect *all the time*.

theme The main musical idea in an **improvisation** or **composition**.

timbre See **tone**.

tone This word has several meanings. Strictly speaking, the word should be used to refer to the quality or character of sound made by *an individual performer* (e.g. Louis Armstrong's tone was different from that of Bix Beiderbecke). However, the word is often used instead of **timbre**, which refers to the quality or character of sound made by a particular instrument, for example the timbre (sound) of a violin, as compared to the timbre (sound) of a trumpet.

twelve-bar blues A musical form which has become the basis of many blues and blues-based jazz compositions and improvisations. It is a **chord sequence** in which the number of **bars** (twelve) and the pattern of **chords** is fixed.

Sources and acknowledgments

P. 11, Civil Code from R. Harris: *Jazz* (Penguin, 1956), p. 23; p. 12, work song from H. W. Odum and G. B. Johnson: *The Negro and his Songs* (University of North Carolina Press, 1925), p. 252; p. 15, spiritual from H. Courlander: *Negro Folk Music, U.S.A.* (Columbia University Press, 1963), p. 42; p. 18, Brownie McGhee from R. Neff and A. Connor: *Blues* (David R. Godine, 1975), p. 1; p. 19, Robert Pete Williams from B. Cook: *Listen to the Blues* (Robson Books, 1975), p. 35; p. 22, Big Bill Broonzy from W. Broonzy: *Big Bill Blues* (Cassell, 1955) pp. 88–9; p. 26, anonymous quote from 'Roots of the Blues' in *The Story of Pop*, vol. 1 (Phoebus Publishing, 1974), p. 39; p. 32, Baby Dodds from N. Shapiro and N. Hentoff: *Hear me Talkin' to ya* (Penguin, 1962), p. 39; p. 34, lyrics of 'High Sheriff Blues' from B. Cook, op. cit., p. 73; p. 35, lyrics from 'High Water Everywhere' from P. Oliver: *The Story of the Blues* (Barrie & Rockliff, 1969), p. 31; p. 38, Blind Lemon Jefferson lyric from Cook, op. cit., p. 105; p. 42, Jimmy McPartland from Shapiro and Hentoff, op. cit., p. 135; p. 44, Louis Armstrong from Shapiro and Hentoff, op. cit., p. 109; p. 49, Mr Clark from N. Leonard: *Jazz and the White Americans* (University of Chicago Press, 1962), p. 37; p. 49, Dr Richards from Leonard, op. cit., p. 39; p. 52, Carr and Blackwell lyric from G. Oakley: *The Devil's Music* (BBC, 1976), p. 176; p. 53, 'Poor Man's Blues' lyric from Oakley, op. cit., p. 108; p. 55, anonymous quote from Shapiro and Hentoff, op. cit., p. 242; p. 59, Rex Stewart from N. Hentoff: *Jazz Is* (Random House, 1976), p. 69; p. 64, anonymous quote from Shapiro and Hentoff, op. cit., p. 221; p. 64, Duke Ellington from a Radio 3 broadcast; p. 68, Lionel Hampton from T. Palmer: *All You Need Is Love* (Futura, 1977), p. 61; p. 68, Roy Eldridge from Shapiro and Hentoff, op. cit.,

pp. 320–1; p. 71, Johnny Shines from Cook, op. cit., p.
133; p. 72, Son House from S. Charters: *The Bluesmen*
(Oak Publications, 1967), p. 99; p. 72, Sammy Price from
M. Stearns: *The Story of Jazz* (Oxford University Press,
1956), p. 135; p. 73, Count Basie from *Melody Maker*, 22
November 1975; p. 78, Thelonious Monk's mother from N.
Hentoff: *The Jazz Life* (Panther, 1964), p. 165; p. 79,
Thelonious Monk from Shapiro and Hentoff, op. cit., p.
330; p. 79, Kenny Clarke from Shapiro and Hentoff, op.
cit., p. 342; p. 83, Earl Hines from Shapiro and Hentoff,
op. cit., p. 340; p. 85, Cootie Williams from N. Hentoff:
Jazz Is, p. 166; p. 85, Thelonious Monk from N. Hentoff:
Jazz Is, p. 146; p. 86, Louis Armstrong from Stearns, op.
cit., pp. 155–6; p. 89, Miles Davis from B. Sidran: *Black
Talk* (Holt, Rinehart & Winston, 1971), p. 138; p. 93,
Archie Shepp from *Downbeat*, vol. 33, no. 10, 19 May
1966, p. 41; p. 94, Cecil Taylor's bass player from N.
Hentoff: *Jazz Is*, p. 233; p. 94, Albert Ayler from
Downbeat, vol. 33, no. 23, pp. 17–40; p. 94, review quote
from Derek Jewell in the *Sunday Times*; p. 100, Muddy
Waters from Cook, op. cit., p. 185; p. 102, Howlin' Wolf
from P. Guralnick: *Feel Like Going Home* (Dutton, 1971),
p. 53; p. 102, Muddy Waters from Guralnick, op. cit., p.
53; p. 104, Muddy Waters lyric from C. Keil: *Urban Blues*
(University of Chicago Press, 1966), p. 72; p. 106, T.
Bone Walker from Oakley, op. cit., p. 232; p. 109, B. B.
King from Oakley, op. cit., pp. 233–4; p. 112, B. B. King
from Cook, op. cit., p. 198; p. 114, Fan's comment from
Keil, op. cit., p. 157; p. 115, B. B. King from Cook, op.
cit., p. 199; p. 117, Louis Jordan from J. S. Roberts: *Black
Music of Two Worlds* (Allen Lane, 1973), p. 221; p. 121,
Gibbs and Ballard lyrics from C. Gillett: *The Sound of the
City* (Sphere, 1971), pp. 24–5; p. 124, Big Bill Broonzy
from M. Haralambos: *Right On: From Blues to Soul in
Black America* (Eddison Press, 1974), p. 101; p. 128, Eric
Clapton from Cook, op. cit., pp. 178–9; p. 128, John
Lennon from A. Shaw: *The Rock Revolution* (Paperback
Library, 1971), p. 26; p. 129, John Lee Hooker from Neff
and Connor, op. cit., p. 121; p. 131, Son House from B.
Groom: *The Blues Revival* (November Books, 1971); pp.
58–9; p. 135, Duke Ellington from N. Hentoff: *Jazz Is*, p.
29; p. 135, Ian Carr from I. Carr: *Music Outside* (Latimer,
1973), p. ix; p. 137, Mance Lipscomb from P. Oliver:
Conversation with the Blues (Cassell, 1965), p. 27; p. 139,
T. Bone Walker from Shapiro and Hentoff, op. cit., p. 246;

p. 139, Alberta Hunter from Shapiro and Hentoff, op. cit., p. 244; p. 140, Sydney Bechet from 'The Black Struggle', *The Story of Pop*, vol. 2, p. 410; p. 140, anonymous quote from V. Wilmer: *Jazz People* (Quartet, 1977), p. 81; p. 141, Howard McGhee from R. Russell: *Bird Lives!* (Quartet, 1973), p. 196.

Pictures   Pp. vi, 2 (below), 36, 62, 70, 93, 98, 101, 103, 107, 108, 110, 113, 120, 123, Bill Greensmith; pp. 21, 31, 47, 54, 61, 67, 81, 84, 125, Jazz Music Books; pp. 15, 28, 75, 133, 138, Valerie Wilmer; pp. 8, 9, 10, 13, the Mansell Collection; pp. 41, 130, Sylvia Pitcher; p. 136, Jak Kilby; p. 7, the Royal Anthropological Institute; p. 2 (above), the Royal Philharmonic Orchestra; p. 74, Alan Johnson; the author and publishers are grateful to the above for permission to reproduce copyright material. Pictures on p. 4 were taken by the author.

Some suggestions for further reading and listening

Books   **Blues**
The two best general books on the history of the blues are:

Giles Oakley: *The Devil's Music: A History of the Blues* (BBC, 1976).
Paul Oliver: *The Story of the Blues* (Barrie & Rockliff, reprinted 1978).

Both are very well illustrated and particularly good on the general social and economic background.
Also recommended are: ˊ

Peter Guralnick: *Feel Like Going Home* (Omnibus Press, 1978).
Bruce Cook: *Listen to the Blues* (Robson Books, 1975).

Both are very readable books on the background and influence of the blues.
An excellent collection of photographs and quotations from blues musicians is to be found in:

Robert Neff and Anthony Connor: *Blues* (David R. Godine, 1975).

Jazz
One of the most readable books on jazz is a history based entirely on quotations from musicians and others connected with the jazz business:

Nat Shapiro and Nat Hentoff: *Hear Me Talkin' To Ya* (Penguin, 1962).

Other very readable introductions are:

J. Berendt: *The Jazz Book* (Paladin, 1976). Excellent value in the paperback edition.

Graham Collier: *Inside Jazz* (Quartet Books, 1973).
Edward Lee: *Jazz: An Introduction* (Stanmore Press, 1972).

Also recommended:

Brian Case and Stan Britt: *The Illustrated Encyclopaedia of Jazz* (Salamander Books, 1978). A very well illustrated A to Z of famous jazz and blues musicians, together with selective discographies.

Recordings **Blues**
Highly recommended as an introduction to the whole range of blues music:

The Story of the Blues, vol. I, CBS.
The Story of the Blues, vol. 2, CBS.

These accompany Paul Oliver's book *The Story of the Blues*.
Two of the most famous rural blues musicians can be heard on:

Charley Patton: *Charley Patton and the Country Blues*, Origin.
Robert Johnson: *King of the Delta Blues Singers*, vol. I, CBS.

Classic blues is well represented on:

Bessie Smith: *The Empress*, CBS.

The different styles of urban blues can be compared on:

Muddy Waters: *The Best of Muddy Waters*, Chess.
B. B. King: *Live at the Regal*, ABC/HMV.

Jazz
Classic New Orleans jazz can be heard on:

King Oliver's Creole Jazz Band 1923, Riverside.

Louis Armstrong's famous recording of 'West End Blues' is on:

Louis Armstrong V.S.O.P., vol. 4, CBS.

Big bands can be heard at their best on:

Count Basie: *Blues I Love to Sing*, Ace of Hearts.
   Featuring also Jimmy Rushing, the blues singer.
Duke Ellington: *Ellington at Newport*, CBS.

Bebop is best represented by the classic recording of a live concert in Massey Hall, Toronto:

Quintet of the Year, Debut/Vogue. Featuring Charlie Parker, Dizzy Gillespie, Charlie Mingus, Bud Powell and Max Roach.

Miles Davis's development towards jazz-rock can be seen from comparing:

Kind of Blue, CBS (1959).
Bitches Brew, CBS (1970).

Free jazz avant-garde can be heard on:

Ornette Coleman: *At the Golden Circle*, Blue Note.
Cecil Taylor: *Unit Structures*, Blue Note.

Index

References to illustrations are in italics at the end of entries.